The Automated Summary Engine

By
Violet

Contents

Chapter 1

Introduction

The objective of this chapter is:

- To introduce the role of automatic text summarization.
- To highlight the challenges in retrieving relevant content from a large corpus.
- To present the objective of this thesis.
- To highlight the contributions that helped achieve the objective.

1.1 Automatic Text Summarization

The web is home to a vast and ever-growing amount of textual content, including websites, user reviews, news articles, blogs, and social media platforms. In addition to this, there are massive text archives containing novels, books, legal records, biomedical documents, and scientific publications. This volume of textual data is expanding rapidly every day. As a result, users often spend considerable time searching for specific information. Even then, they are unable to read or process all the content returned by search engines, much of which is repetitive or irrelevant. Given this overload of information, there is a growing need to summarize and distill textual resources efficiently. However, creating summaries manually is both time-consuming and labor-intensive. In reality, it's nearly impossible for humans to keep up with summarizing such a large-scale corpus of information [1]. This is where Automatic Text Summarization (ATS) emerges as a practical and powerful solution to the problem. The primary goal of an ATS system is to generate a concise version of a document that captures its core ideas while minimizing redundancy [2, 3]. These systems enable users to quickly grasp the essential points of a document without having to read it in its entirety [4]. By delivering summaries automatically, ATS systems help users save significant time and effort, making information consumption more efficient. ATS systems can be generally categorized as single-document and multi-document summarization. Single-document summarization focuses on generating a summary from an individual document, whereas multi-document summarization creates a unified summary by combining and condensing information from a group of related documents.

1.1.1 Uses of summarization

There are several notable benefits of automatic text summarization, as outlined below:

- **Saves time and effort:** Summarization significantly reduces the time and effort required to process large volumes of text. Users can quickly grasp the main ideas without having to read the entire content.
- **Enhances focus:** By filtering out unnecessary details, summarization helps users concentrate on the most important information, reducing cognitive overload and improving attention.
- **Facilitates learning:** Summaries make it easier to retain key information and concepts. They enable quicker revision and long-term recall, which is particularly useful in reviewing.
- **Improves communication:** Summarized content is concise and to the point, making it easier to share and explain to others. This enhances clarity and speeds up the communication process.
- **Supports faster decision-making:** With quick access to the core information, users can make informed decisions more efficiently. Summaries provide a clear overview of the situation, aiding in better judgment.
- **Widely applicable:** Text summarization is widely used in domains such as journalism, academic research, legal analysis, and business reportsanywhere concise understanding of complex text is needed.

TABLE 1.1: Example showing the output of both ETS and AbTS approaches.

Text corpus	
There was an old owl who lived in an oak tree. Every day, he observed incidents that occurred around him. Today, he saw a young girl shouting at her mother. The more he saw, the less he spoke. As the days went on, he spoke less but heard more. But the old owl in the tree had become wiser, each and every day.	
Extractive summary	**Abstractive summary**
There was an old owl who lived in an oak tree. Today, he saw a young girl shouting at her mother. As the days went on, he spoke less but heard more.	An ancient owl used to reside in an oak tree. He observed a young child yelling at her mother today. He spoke less but heard more as the days passed.

1.1.2 Approaches to Automatic Text Summarization

Automatic text summarization (ATS) methods are generally divided into two main categories: (i) extractive text summarization (ETS) [5] and (ii) abstractive text summarization (AbTS) [6]. The primary distinction between these approaches lies in the nature of the generated output. An example illustrating this difference is provided in Table 1.1.

Extractive text summarization (ETS) involves selecting and extracting the most significant sentences or phrases from the original text to form a summary. The extracted sentences are typically chosen based on their relevance, importance, and coherence. This method rearranges the chosen sentences to create a logical summary while maintaining the precise phrasing from the original text. Various techniques exist for handling extractive summarization: including methods like XSumm-PSO [7] and XSumm-TenAF [8]. On the other hand, abstractive text summarization (AbTS) generates a more "human" like summary that conveys the most important information from the original text after understanding the meaning of the text. The resulting summary may contain sentences that were not present in the original text. Various techniques exist for handling abstractive summarization: including methods like Pre-training with Extracted Gap-sentences for Abstractive SUmmarization S (PEGASUS) [9, 10] and mT5 (mT5-multilingual-XLSum) [11] models are fined-tuned for this approaches.

In real-world scenarios, practical applications of ATS include news summarization tools like Newsblaster [12] and ASFuL [12], which automatically generate summaries of text. Newsblaster helps users find the most desirable news to them and ASFul is an aspect-based sentiment summarization system. Compared to the abstractive summarization (AbTS) , the ETS is simpler and faster. Since the sentences are directly extracted using this method, users can read the summary using the same terminology as in the original text.

1.2 Challenges associated with usages of automatic text summarization

Summarization remains a persistent challenge in generating concise and coherent summaries from textual data, despite the implementation of various policies aimed at its mitigation. Extensive research on this task has been presented in the literature review (Chapter 2). We have oberseved some challenges for text summarization from the chapter 2: **(1) Scarcity of Annotated Datasets:** Most Indian languages lack large, high-quality, manually annotated datasets for summarization, making supervised and deep learning approaches difficult to train and evaluate. We can see in example, "while English has datasets like CNN/DailyMail for summarization, languages such as Tamil or Telugu lack large, publicly available document-summary pairs, forcing researchers to rely on small or manually created datasets", **(2) Rich Morphological Complexity:** Indian languages exhibit complex inflectional and agglutinative morphology, which increases vocabulary size and complicates sentence representation, feature extraction, and semantic similarity estimation. Example is shown in Figure. 1.1, **(3) Limited Linguistic Resources and Tools:** Essential NLP tools such as robust tokenizers, stemmers, lemmatizers, POS taggers, and dependency parsers are either unavailable or unreliable for many Indian languages. We can also see in example "Reliable POS taggers or dependency parsers are unavailable or inaccurate for languages like Gujarati or Hindi, leading to poor sentence segmentation and incorrect importance scoring during summarization, **(4) Orthographic and Script Variations:** Multiple scripts, spelling variations, and inconsistent orthographic conventions introduce noise that negatively impacts sentence scoring and summary coherence. Here is a proper, concrete example with two Bengali sentences that clearly shows the problem and is suitable for an academic paper in Fig 1.2, **(5) Noisy and Informal Text:** The prevalence of spelling errors, transliterations, abbreviations, and informal contractions reduces sentence informativeness and affects summary quality, **(6) Code-Mixing and Code-Switching:** Frequent mixing of English with Indian languages in real-world text (e.g., social media, news comments) complicates sentence segmentation and semantic interpretation, **(7) Lack of Evaluation Benchmarks:** Standardized evaluation datasets and metrics tailored to Indian languages are limited, making fair comparison and reproducibility challenging. For example, we can see that standard evaluation metrics like ROUGE rely on reference summaries, which are rarely available for Indian languages, making it difficult to objectively evaluate summarization performance, **(8) Language Bias in Existing Models:** Most summarization models are designed and optimized for high-resource languages (e.g., English), leading to poor generalization when applied to Indian languages. We can see in example "Summarization models trained on English datasets often fail to capture the syntactic and semantic structures of Malayalam or Kannada, resulting in incomplete or incoherent summaries", **(9) Semantic Representation Limitations:-** Pretrained embeddings and language models often inadequately capture semantic nuances of Indian languages due to insufficient training data. **Example:** Pretrained word embeddings for Gujarati may not capture subtle semantic differences between words, leading to inaccurate sentence similarity and redundancy in summaries, **(10) Handling Long and Complex Sentences:-** Indian languages often employ long, syntactically complex sentence structures, which makes sentence segmentation and importance estimation difficult. **Example:** In Telugu, sentences are often long and clause-rich. A single sentence may contain multiple ideas, making it difficult for extractive summarization methods to identify key information.

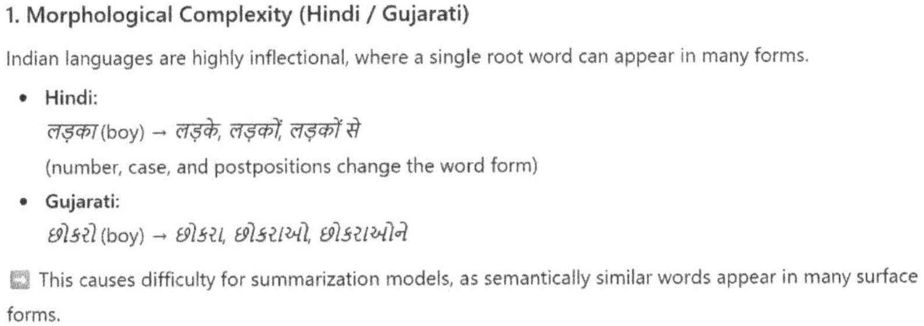

1. Morphological Complexity (Hindi / Gujarati)

Indian languages are highly inflectional, where a single root word can appear in many forms.

- **Hindi:**
  लड़का (boy) → *लड़के, लड़कों, लड़कों से*
  (number, case, and postpositions change the word form)
- **Gujarati:**
  છોકરો (boy) → *છોકરા, છોકરાઓ, છોકરાઓને*

This causes difficulty for summarization models, as semantically similar words appear in many surface forms.

FIGURE 1.1: Morphological complexity in low resource languages

Current models face significant challenges in generating summaries in Indian languages due to a lack of resources. Our research focuses on generating summaries

Sentence 1:
বাংলাদেশ সরকার নতুন নীতি ঘোষণা করেছে।

Sentence 2:
বাংলাদেশ সরকার নতুন নীতি ঘোষনা করেছে।

In this example, the words "**ঘোষণা**" and "**ঘোষনা**" have different spellings but the **same meaning**. However, a summarization system that relies on surface-level token matching will treat them as **distinct tokens**, leading to a **lower sentence similarity score**, even though the sentences are semantically identical.

FIGURE 1.2: Orthographic and Script variation complexity in low resource languages

from low-resource languages, and addressing issues related to spelling errors, code mixing, and grammatical correctness, semantic representation, morphological complexity in exiting methods.

Concluding the above discussion, we identified the following key research gaps (RG):

- RG 1 There is a lack of comprehensive research on leveraging graph-based features and supervised ranking models to capture semantic representations and reduce morphological complexity for low-resource languages such as Hindi and Gujarati.
- RG 2 Despite their effectiveness in high-resource settings, statistical and linguistic features have received limited attention in low-resource Indian language contexts.
- RG 3 Despite their potential importance, supervised optimization frameworks and features related to spelling errors and grammatical correctness have received limited attention in prior work.
- RG 4 Despite their success in English abstractive summarization, transformer models have shown limited generalization to low-resource variants such as Indian English, especially under conditions of increased morphological complexity and code-mixing.

Addressing these challenges are crucial to improving the effectiveness of both extractive and abstractive summarization methods. Despite substantial progress in summary generation, notable limitations remain, thereby motivating the development of more innovative and effective models to address these challenges.

1.3 Objectives

These challenges have motivated the development of effective methods for automatic text summarization (ATS), leveraging both extractive and abstractive approaches for single-document summarization across multiple languages.
To address this, the following four specific objectives are pursued:

Obj. 1 To design a system for generating error free, and more coherent extractive summary using a supervised PSO and dynamic PSO framework by introducing an Incorrect word and Fluency Score for enhanced accuracy, as motivated by RG 3

Obj. 2 To design a system for generating the extractive summary using machine learning (ML) regression models with Node2Vec feature, as motivated by RG 1.

Obj. 3 To design a system for generating extractive summary using statistical, and linguistic features for low resource Indian languages, as motivated by RG 2.

Obj. 4 To develop an encoder-decoder-based system for generating abstractive summaries specifically tailored to the Indian English language, as motivated by RG 4.

1.4 Contribution

To achieve the stated objectives, a range of models – including deep learning, optimization, and machine learning techniques – have been proposed for processing textual content. An overview of the overall contributions is illustrated in the accompanying Figure 1.3. To address the first objective, two text-based extractive summarization models have been developed in Chapter 3. These models utilize both static and dynamic Particle Swarm Optimization (PSO) techniques in a supervised framework to generate coherent, and error-free summaries for English language. Feature extraction from the textual data is performed using a combination of statistical and linguistic features, along with two newly introduced features: "Incorrect word and "Fluency Score" . To address the second objective in Chapter 4, machine learning (ML) regression models leveraging graph-based features have been proposed to generate extractive summaries for single-document inputs in Hindi and Gujarati languages. To achieve the third objective in Chapter 5, statistical and linguistic features have been employed to extract meaningful information from textual data, enabling the generation of extractive summaries in different low-resource Indian languages. To achieve the fourth objective in Chapter 6, an encoder-decoder transformer-based model has been proposed for generating abstractive summaries in Indian English. Word2Vec has been used to extract features from the textual content for semantic representation.

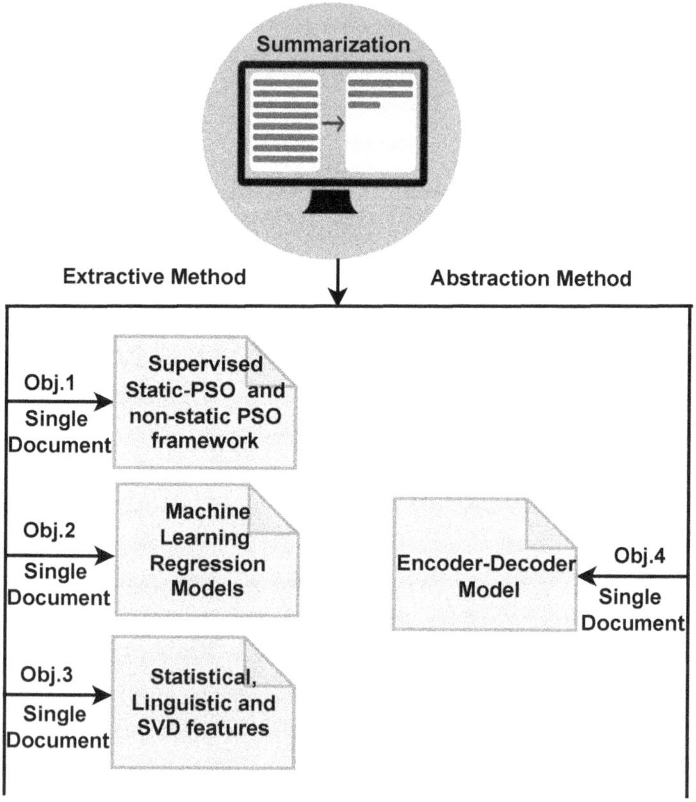

FIGURE 1.3: Flow diagram for the proposed systems

1.4.1 Extractive summrization using supervised PSO framework under Obj. 1

The proposed text-based extractive summarization system, developed in a supervised manner, is organized into two distinct methods: (1) Summaries generated using Static Particle Swarm Optimization (PSO) (see Figure 1.4), and (2) Summaries generated using Non-static PSO (see Figure 1.5).

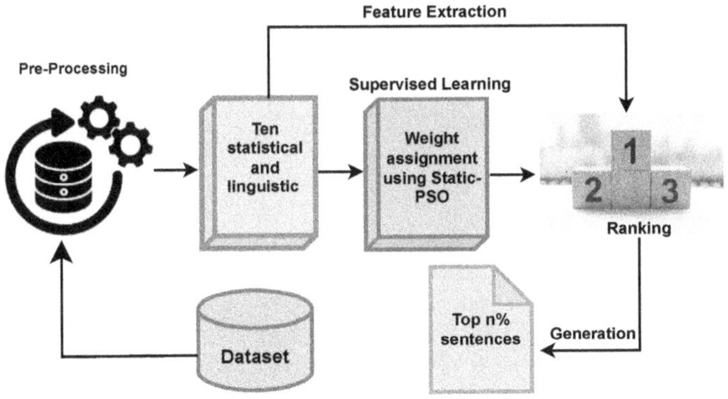

FIGURE 1.4: Process flow of extractive summarization using static PSO in a supervised setting

At the outset of the first method, the pre-processing phase involved and following this, a total of ten features were extracted from each sentence, which served as input for the PSO-based summarization models. These features include: (1) Sentence Length, (2) Sentence Position, (3) Numeric Data , (4) Thematic Words, (5) TF-ISF (Term FrequencyInverse Sentence Frequency), (6) Aggregation Score, (7) Named Entity Recognition , (8) Part-of-Speech (POS) tags focusing on nouns and verbs, (9) Entropy, and (10) Incorrect word . Among these ten features, nine are based on existing approaches, while one novel feature Incorrect word has been newly introduced in this study. The incorrect word feature is designed to detect erroneous or malformed words, thereby helping the system avoid selecting such sentences in the final summary and ensuring the production of error-free summaries. These ten features were provided as input to the static PSO algorithm operating in a continuous domain, which was used to optimize sentence rankings based on the relevance of the features. The PSO algorithm iteratively updates

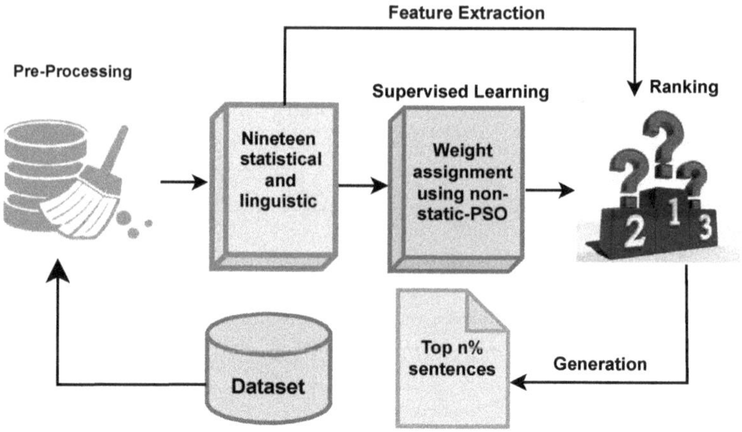

FIGURE 1.5: Process flow of extractive summarization using non-static PSO in a supervised setting

sentence scores based on a fitness function until an optimal combination of feature weights is determined for sentence selection.

Building on this foundation, the work was extended in three significant ways in the second method: (i) By incorporating an enhanced set of features beyond the initial ten, (ii) By introducing a new feature named Fluency Score , and (iii) By implementing a non-static PSO variant capable of adapting its optimization strategy dynamically during execution. The enhanced feature set now includes nine additional features, numbered from 11 to 19: (11) Busy Path, (12) TextRank Score, (13) Lexical Similarity , (14) Word Co-occurrence, (15) Cue Words , (16) Title Match Feature, (17) Upper Case Count, (18) Term Weight, and (19) Fluency Score . The Fluency score feature is particularly noteworthy. It is a metric that evaluates how well a sentence adheres to the rules of grammar, syntactic structure, and overall readability. It estimates how natural a sentence sounds to a native speaker or language model. This feature helps prioritize sentences that are naturally well-formed and easy to understand. It helps prevent the inclusion of noisy or low-quality sentences in the generated summary after sentence scoring.

These nineteen features were then fed into the non-static PSO algorithm, also operating in a continuous domain. Unlike static PSO, the non-static variant adapts its velocity and position update mechanisms over time, offering improved convergence behavior and enhanced adaptability to diverse feature sets. The goal, as in the static case, is to optimize the sentence ranking based on the combined relevance of all features.

A detailed explanation of both static and non-static PSO-based summarization models, including the mathematical formulations, feature engineering strategies, and performance analysis, is provided in Chapter 3.

1.4.2 Extractive summrization using ML regression models under Obj. 2

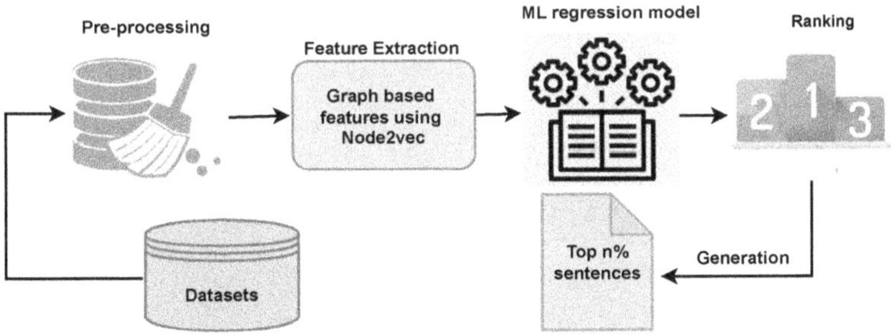

FIGURE 1.6: Process flow of extractive summarization using Machine Learning regression models

The text-based extractive summarization system is developed using machine learning (ML) regression models. The overall architecture and workflow of the proposed system are illustrated in Figure 1.6. At the start of the work, a pre-processing of the text is performed and Node2Vec algorithm is applied to transform the document into a graph-based structure, from which sentence-level features are extracted in the form of dense vector embeddings and serve as input features. In the text summarization task, reference summaries act as annotations linked to the original article. However, to train regression models, these summaries must be transformed into a numerical format. To achieve this, we utilized Word Movers Distance (WMD) to measure the similarity between each sentence in the article and each sentence in the reference summary. We then fed these features into eight ML regression models named: (1) Support vector regression (SVR); (2) Linear regression (LR); (3) K-neighbors regressor (KNR); (4) Random forest regressor

(RFR); (5) Bayesian Ridge (BR); (6) Gradient boosting regressor (GBR); (7) Decision tree regressor (DTR); (8) AdaBoost regressor (ABR) to generate the summaries. Each model learns to predict the importance of sentences based on their features, and the top-ranked sentences are selected to form the extractive summary. The proposed model is evaluated on datasets in Hindi and Gujarati from the FIRE-2022 shared task on Indian Languages Summarization (ILSUM). A detailed explanation of the methodology, experimental setup, regression models, and results is provided in Chapter 4.

1.4.3 Extractive summrization using statistical and linguistic features under Obj. 3

Two distinct models have been proposed for generating extractive summaries tailored to low-resource Indian languages using monolingual textual data.
For the first model (see Figure 1.7), a pre-processing of the text is performed and the model constructs ten distinct statistical and linguistic features, each designed to capture different aspects of sentence importance. These features are: (1) Sentence Length, (2) Sentence Position, (3) Numeric Data, (4) Thematic Words, (5) Entropy, (6) POS tags (noun, verb), (7) TF-ISF, (8) Aggregation Score, (9) Busy Path, and (10) Title Match . Once these features are computed for all sentences in the document, they are aggregatedby summing their normalized valuesto assign an importance score to each sentence. The top-ranked sentences are then selected to form the extractive summary. This model has been tested on datasets in Hindi and English, both of which are part of the Indian linguistic landscape, to validate the effectiveness of the feature-based scoring mechanism in both resource-rich and low-resource conditions.

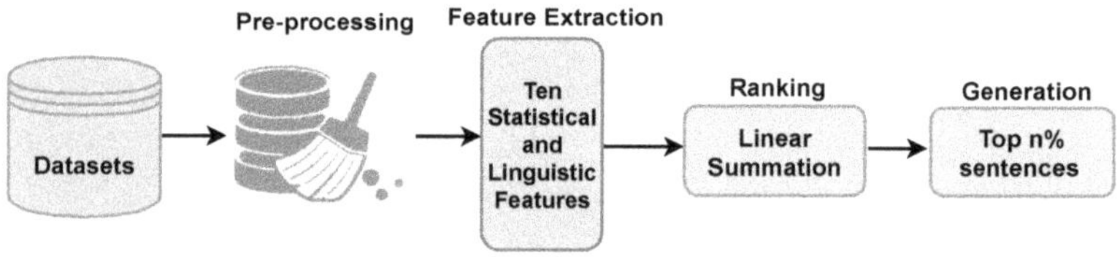

FIGURE 1.7: Flow diagram of extractive model using statistical and linguistic features

The second model (as shown in Figure 1.8) also initiates with pre-processing of the input text. It employs the Term Frequency Inverse Document Frequency (TF-IDF) method to convert sentences into vector representations. After vectorization, the model applies the Singular Value Decomposition (SVD) algorithm, a well-known dimensionality reduction technique, to uncover latent semantic structures and extract the most informative components from the sentence vectors. Similar to the first model, all the derived features are combined by computing their aggregate scores across the sequence of sentences, and the highest scoring sentences are selected to generate the summary. The proposed model is evaluated on datasets of five Indian languages named: Telugu, Tamil, Gujarati, Hindi and Bengali.

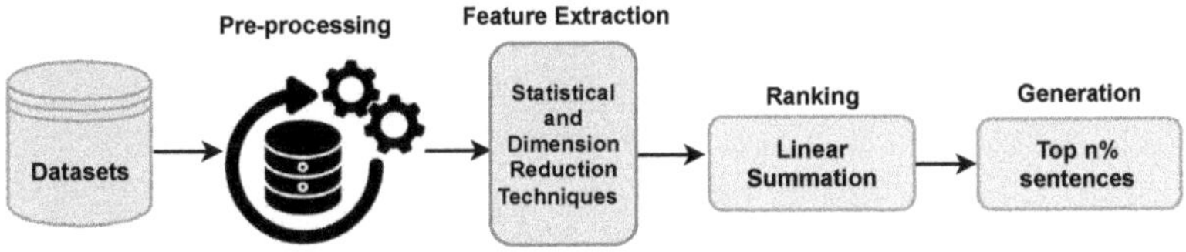

FIGURE 1.8: Flow diagram of extractive model using Statistical and dimension reduction techniques

A detailed overview of both models, including their architectural designs, feature engineering strategies, preprocessing pipelines, evaluation protocols, and experimental outcomes, is presented in Chapter 5. The chapter also elaborates on how these models address the limitations posed by low-resource language settings and the comparative analysis of their performance across multiple languages.

1.4.4 Abstractive summrization using sequence-to-sequence (Seq2Seq) model for Indian English under Obj. 4

The abstractive summarization system is developed by sequence-to-sequence (Seq2Seq) model. The Seq2Seq model comprises two essential components: (1) an encoder and (2) a decoder. A comprehensive flow diagram illustrating the architecture and operation of the proposed model is depicted in Figure 1.9. A pre-processing of the text is performed and Word2Vec model is applied to convert words into vectors form. The encoder is responsible for processing the input sequence-typically a sentence or document-by converting it into an internal representation, which is often a fixed-size or variable-length context vector. This context encapsulates the semantic and syntactic structure of the input. The decoder, on the other hand, utilizes this encoded context to generate the output sequence in a step-by-step manner, typically forming the target summary in an abstractive format. The proposed summarization system is specifically evaluated on an Indian English dataset, sourced from the Forum for Information Retrieval Evaluation (FIRE-2022) shared task on ILSUM . In this work, we addressed factual inaccuracy and linguistic challenges unique to Indian English, improving over standard Seq2Seq and transformer models trained on generic English corpora. Chapter 6 provides a detailed explanation of the systems architecture, the underlying methodology, training strategies, and the evaluation metrics employed. The chapter also discusses experimental results and highlights the impact of using contextual embeddings and attention-based decoding in improving summary coherence and relevance.

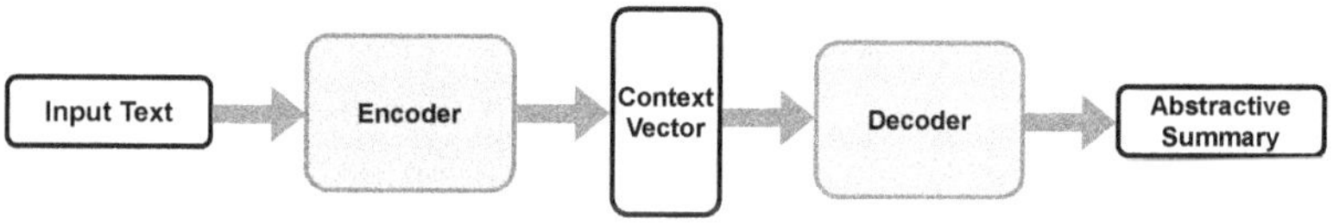

FIGURE 1.9: Flow diagram of abstractive summarization using encoder-decoder model

1.5 Impact of this research-both academic (methodological contribution) and practical (applications in multilingual summarization systems)

Academically, the thesis contributes novel methodologies for extractive and abstractive summarization, including two new features representations, supervised PSO, ML regression models, and encoder-decoder architectures specifically tailored for low-resource Indian languages and Indian English. This additionally utilizes existing features specifically designed for low-resource languages. Practically, the proposed methods have the potential to enhance multilingual summarization systems, enabling more accurate, fluent, and culturally coherent summaries across diverse domains, thereby supporting applications in news aggregation, social media analysis, and knowledge management for underrepresented languages.

1.6 Organization of thesis

The rest of the thesis is organized as follows:

- Chapter 2 provides a comprehensive review of existing literature on extractive and abstractive single-document summarization. It examines both supervised and unsupervised approaches to text summarization and identifies key research gaps in the current body of work. The chapter also introduces the datasets and evaluation metrics employed to assess the performance of the proposed models.
- Chapter 3 emphasizes the need for an automatic summarization system capable of generating accurate, error-free extractive summaries. It introduces a supervised optimization technique and explores the effectiveness of incorporating novel features such as Incorrect word and Fluency Score in enhancing summarization performance.
- Chapter 4 presents the need for an automatic summarization system to generate extractive summaries, whereby several ML models designed to predict sentence scores based on graph-based sentence features are presented. Additionally, it discusses the effectiveness of two different models-Word2Vec and Node2Vec-for extracting meaningful features from document content.
- Chapter 5 highlights the need for generating extractive summaries using statistical and linguistic techniques from various low-resource Indian monolingual languages. It presents its performance is evaluated against other models.
- Chapter 6 presents the need for generating abstractive summary from Indian English mono-lingual language. It presents encoder-decoder tansformer-based method, and its performance is evaluated against other models.
- Chapter 7 provides an overview of the main contributions of the thesis, discusses its limitations, and suggests avenues for future research.

Chapter 2

Literature Review, Datasets and Evaluation metrices

The objective of this chapter is:

1. To introduce state-of-the art methods proposed by researchers for the effective use of large textual data for automatic summarization.

2. To present the various evaluation metrics employed to assess the performance of the proposed models.

3. To present the datasets utilized for validating the performance of the proposed models.

This chapter presents state-of-the-art approaches [13–17] proposed by various researchers for automatic text summarization of large-scale textual data. To systematically organize the literature, this section is divided into two subsections: (1) extractive summarization and (2) abstractive summarization. The performance of these summarization approaches is evaluated using various evaluation metrics, and different benchmark datasets are employed to validate the effectiveness of the proposed models. Details of these evaluation strategies and datasets are discussed in this chapter.

2.0.1 Extractive Summarization

Extractive summarization is a summarization technique in which a summary is generated by selecting and concatenating the most important sentences or phrases directly from the original document, without modifying their wording. Existing research has explored several classical summarization approaches, including statistical, graph-based, optimization-based, and machine learning-based methods. The techniques corresponding to each approach are discussed in detail in the following sections.

1) Statistical-based approaches: One of the first automatic summarization systems, using word frequency statistics and heuristics to identify important sentences by Luhn et al. [18]. Early rule/statistical based method that influenced many later approaches. To raise the quality of the generated summary, Edmundson et al. [19] expanded on Lunh's work by adding these features: word frequency, title word, sentence position, and cue phrases in the documents. Further, this approach utilizes a range of statistical and linguistic features to rank sentences for summary generation. These features include: Sentence length [14, 20], sentence position [14, 20], sentence similarity [14], sentences with frequent words [14], sentences with numerical data [7, 14, 20, 21], named entity recognition [7, 21], title similarity [20, 21], topic modeling (Latent Dirichlet Allocation (LDA)) [21], term frequency [22], term frequency-inverse sentence frequency [22], word co-occurrence [22], proper noun [22], bushy path [22], entropy [7], latent semantic analysis [22], Thematic words [7, 20], cue words [22], aggregate similarity [7, 23], lexical similarity [23], and upper case [23]. Oliveira et al.[5] utilized eighteen different sentence scoring methods to determine the significance of a sentence for the summarization task. Meena et al. [22] proposed a sentence ranking approach based on reciprocal ranking to effectively prioritize sentences for summarization. Dhankhar et al. [24] introduced different combinations by using nine statistical features to compute the sentence score. Ferreira et al. [23] focuses on extractive summarization with fifteen-sentence scoring methods employing both quantitative and qualitative evaluation methods. Hark et al. [25] introduce Karci Summarization as a straightforward and efficient method for automatic text summarization utilizing Karci entropy. Singh et al. [8] extracted features from each sentence in the document using ten statistical features, and then summed these features to score sentences for both Hindi and English languages to generate the summary. Mohamed et al. [26] proposed an approach based on semantic role labelling (SRL) and explicit semantic analysis (ESA) summarization, integrating both single-document summarization and multi-document summarization. Gong et al. [17] proposed two unsupervised methods for generic extractive text summarization. The first method computes sentence relevance scores using standard information retrieval (IR) techniques and iteratively selects the most representative sentences while reducing redundancy through term elimination. The second method applies Latent Semantic Analysis (LSA) [17] via Singular Value Decomposition (SVD) to identify sentences that best represent the dominant semantic concepts in a document. Both methods aim to select diverse, highly ranked sentences that comprehensively cover key document topics. The study also examined the effect of different vector space model (VSM) weighting schemes and found that binary weighting without normalization provided the best results. Patel et al. [27] presented a fuzzy logic-based extractive framework for multi-document summarization, aimed at tackling the limitations of traditional statistical methods-particularly uncertain feature weighting and redundancy. It uses a range of sentence features, including TF-IDF, title words, thematic terms, and sentence position, which are evaluated through a fuzzy inference system with 273 human-crafted rules to assign importance scores. The system then selects and orders sentences while removing redundant ones using cosine similarity, resulting in coherent and diverse summaries. Furthermore, for summarization, the two-tiered topic model based on the pachinko allocation model (PAM) is combined with the TextRank method [16]. To capture the sparse candidate topics under that low-rank matrix factorization model, a novel neighbourhood preserving semantic (NPS) measure was introduced. Kumari et al. [28] introduced an extractive text summarization method employing K-means clustering for the ILSUM-2022 dataset. The technique comprises text tokenization, Word2Vec-based word and sentence vectorization, and dimensionality reduction using autoencoders and K-means clustering. This process facilitates the identification and extraction of key sentences and phrases, generating a coherent and informative summary. While using statistical features alone may not be sufficient [5, 23], combining them with other techniques can improve the outcome.

2) Graph-based approaches: In this approach, summarization methods represent the document as graph having nodes and edges. Nodes are words and sentences in the document. Edges which describe the similarity relations between the text units, such as, cosine similarity, the longest common subsequences, and the number of common words. Graph-based methods like TextRank [29] and LexRank [30], Centroid-based summarization [31], and Lexical Chains [32] model have been widely adopted. Davoodijam et al. [33] employed a multi-layer graph for multiple features using word similarity, semantic similarity, and co-reference similarity. They used MultiRank algorithm for ranking the sentences. Umair et al. [34] proposed N-GPETS (Neural Attention Graph-Based Pretrained Statistical Model), a hybrid extractive summarization framework that integrates pre-trained language models with graph-based learning and statistical features. The model constructs a heterogeneous graph comprising sentence and semantic word nodes, initialized using a combination of BERT embeddings and TF-IDF scores. Graph Attention Networks (GATs) are applied to propagate semantic and contextual information across nodes, enabling enhanced sentence representations for summary extraction.

Zhao et al. [35] proposed multi-granularity heterogeneous graph for text using three different node types: words, sentences, and topics, which are updated by graph attention network. Zhao et al. [36] employed a robust architecture for extractive summarization that constructs a multi-granularity heterogeneous graph, going beyond traditional sentence-only graphs. It effectively captures varying semantic levels-sentences, keyphrases, and topics-producing richer, context-aware summaries. El-Kassas et al. [37] introduce EdgeSumm, a comprehensive unsupervised framework for single-document extractive summarization that synergizes multiple methodologies - statistical, centrality-based, graph-based, and semantic - to overcome the limitations of individual approache. Fang et al. [38] introduced an innovative word-sentence co-ranking model called CoRank, which integrates the word-sentence relationships with a graph-based unsupervised ranking model. Vo et al. [39] introduced SEMantic-aware Feature for Extractive Summarization (SE4ExSum) model integrates multiple components to enhance extractive summarization. First, it constructs a Feature Graph-of-Words (FGOW) to capture local lexical-semantic relationships and encode phrase-level structures. A BERT-based encoder is then employed to generate contextual sentence embeddings. These embeddings, combined with the FGOW, are processed through a Graph Convolutional Network (GCN), which models global semantic and structural relationships within the document.

Finally, the enriched sentence representations are ranked, allowing the model to identify and extract the most salient sentences for summary generation. Mihalcea et al. [29] proposed textRank, an unsupervised graph-based ranking algorithm inspired by PageRank, applied to two natural langauge processing (NLP) tasks: keyword extraction and sentence extraction (summarization). Dong et al. [40] employed a two-phase extractive summarization framework for multi-document inputs. In Phase 1, a Bidirectional Gated Recurrent Unit (Bi-GRU) with content-attention mechanism detects latent sub-topics by capturing semantic relationships across sentences. In Phase 2, key sentences are selected based on their sub-topic relevance and importance scores, ensuring diverse, non-redundant summaries. Praveen et al. [41] introduced an unsupervised extractive summarization method using a weighted topical graph built with LDA-based topic modeling. Sentences and topics form a bi-partite graph, with edge weights reflecting topic-word probabilities. Sentence importance is computed using the Hyperlink-Induced Topic Search (HITS) algorithm, while topical coherence is assessed via a weighted one-mode projection. An Integer Linear Programming (ILP)-based optimization selects sentences that maximize importance, coherence, and topic coverage (to reduce redundancy). Fang et al. [38] proposed CoRank, an unsupervised graph-based extractive summarization method that jointly ranks sentences and words by leveraging their mutual influence. Unlike traditional methods like TextRank, CoRank integrates word-sentence relationships into sentence scoring, enhancing summary quality. An improved version, CoRank+, adds a redundancy elimination step to avoid selecting similar sentences.

3) Optimization-based approaches: In this approach, recognizing the limitations of single-feature summarization models, Jain et al.[21] introduced a Bayesian Optimization-based Score Fusion framework aimed at enhancing extractive summarization of legal documents. Recognizing that legal texts exhibit considerable length and complexity, the authors combine multiple linguistic sentence-scoring methods-spanning both statistical and semantic techniques-and optimize their weighting using Bayesian Optimization to maximize summarization performance. Tanfouri et al. [42] proposed an extractive summarization framework for Arabic text, utilizing a genetic algorithm to optimize sentence selection. The objective function combines two key metrics: term frequency-based sentence scoring and Jaccard similarity. This approach leverages the strengths of both metrics to identify the most relevant sentences for summarization.

Wilson et al. [43] proposed a novel method for multi-document summarization that integrates Sequential Minimal Optimization (SMO) with softmax regression. Their approach leverages both syntactic and semantic features, which are extracted using techniques such as longest common subsequence, n-gram analysis, word order similarity, knowledge-based attributes, and Sen2Vec sentence embeddings. Debnath et al. [44] proposed an approach using an adaptive binary constrained differential evolution algorithm within a multi-objective optimization framework. This approach leverages statistical features: content coverage, sentence position, thematic relevance, length compactness, cohesion, and redundancy minimization to optimize the summarization task. Mishra et al. [45] introduce a novel framework for scientific document summarization that leverages a multi-objective clustering approach optimized via Differential Evolution (DE). The method unfolds in two stages: (1) Citation contextualization is used to extract semantically important sentences from scholarly articles, and (2) sentences are clustered using a multi-objective clustering strategy that simultaneously maximizes cluster compactness and separation, as measured by Pakhira-Bandyopadhyay-Maulik (PBM) and XieBeni (XB) indices, across citation-context-derived clusters. A multi-objective Differential Evolution (MODE) algorithm optimizes these objectives, providing a Pareto-optimal set of sentence clusters from which representative sentences are selected for the summary.

Jain et al. [46] an extractive summarization system specifically designed for Hindi (health domain), using a Real-Coded Genetic Algorithm (RCGA) to optimize sentence scoring. The pipeline includes five main phases: text preprocessing, feature extraction, genetic processing, sentence ranking, and summary generation. Feature extraction incorporates both TF-ISF (a sentence-level variant of TF-IDF) and named-entity and sentence-similarity metrics, producing top-performing feature combinations. RCGA evolves real-valued chromosomes representing feature weights using simulated binary crossover and polynomial mutation, optimizing these weights. During summary generation, sentences with highest scores based on the optimized weights are selected under configurable compression rates. Abuobieda et al. [20] introduced a hybrid method for extractive single-document summarization that utilizes a pseudo-genetic algorithm for feature selection. The approach focuses on five commonly statistical features named Sentence Position, TFISF, Title Similarity, Sentence Length, and Proper Noun Count were selected from the above and encoded as binary genes in a chromosome. Priya et al. [47] proposed an extractive review summarization framework using a multi-objective particle swarm optimization (MOPSO) approach. Their method incorporates both discrete (d-MOPSO) and continuous (c-MOPSO) variants of PSO, effectively combining feature selection, sentiment analysis, and diversity preservation. The framework begins by converting review texts into feature vectors using Bag-of-Words (BoW) and real-valued representations, followed by feature extraction techniques such as Latent Semantic Analysis (LSA) and TF-IDF. To capture sentiment information, a maximum entropy model is used to identify opinion-rich features. The PSO algorithms are driven by customized multi-objective fitness functions that consider both feature importance (through TF-IDF scores) and sentence novelty (based on similarity measures), ensuring the generation of summaries that are both informative and non-redundant. DeepSumm approach leverages the power of both topic models and sequence-to-sequence networks [48]. Topic models are employed to capture the underlying themes in the text, while sequence-to-sequence networks are used to generate extractive summaries. Saini et al. [49] propose a novel approach for extractive microblog summarization in the context of disaster events, formulating the task as a multi-objective optimization problem. The framework employs a self-adaptive Multi-Objective Binary Differential Evolution (MOBDE) algorithm to select a representative subset of tweets by simultaneously optimizing three objectives: maximizing syntactic relevance (TF-IDF score), minimizing redundancy (using Word Mover Distance or Best Match 25 (BM25) similarity), and maximizing tweet length. Three versions of the optimization strategy-MOOTS1 (self-adaptive parameters), MOOTS2 (composite DE variants), and MOOTS3 (hybrid of both)-are introduced. The use of a Self-Organizing Map (SOM)-based genetic operator further enhances solution diversity and convergence. Debnath et al. [50] introduced ETS-MBCSO, a Modified Binary Cat Swarm Optimization-based framework for extractive single-document summarization. The approach optimizes summaries based on content coverage, informativeness, and anti-redundancy using seven sentence-level features, including TF-IDF with n-gram and similarity metrics. Feature scaling ensures balanced feature contribution. Each candidate summary is encoded as a binary vector, and the optimization process uses seeking and tracing strategies guided by an objective function under summary length constraints.

Saini et al. [51] proposed three novel extractive single-document summarization (ESDS) methods based on multi-objective optimization frameworks: self-organized multi-objective differential evolution (ESDS_SMODE), multi-objective grey wolf optimizer (ESDS_MGWO), and multi-objective water cycle algorithm

(ESDS_MWCA). These methods formulate summarization as a sentence clustering problem, where sentence clusters are automatically discovered using compactness and separation-based cluster validity indices (PBM and Xie-Beni). Each sentence is semantically represented using Word2Vec embeddings, and similarity is computed using Word Mover's Distance (WMD) to better capture semantic relevance. Summary sentences are selected from clusters based on features like sentence position, length, similarity to title, and redundancy. Thi et al. [52] proposed a hybrid optimization algorithm, PSOGA-BKSum, which combines Particle Swarm Optimization (PSO) and Genetic Algorithm (GA) for extractive single-document text summarization. While traditional evolutionary algorithms like GA and PSO have shown effectiveness in sentence selection, each has limitations: GA suffers from slow convergence, and PSO is prone to local optima. PSOGA-BKSum integrates the fast convergence of PSO with GA's population diversity, enhancing solution quality. Sentences are represented via TF-IDF in a vector space, and summary fitness is assessed using a linear combination of features: sentence position, similarity to the topic sentence, length, and number of proper nouns. Al-Radaideh et al. [53] introduced a novel hybrid method for Arabic single-document extractive summarization that integrates domain-specific knowledge with statistical features and genetic algorithms (ASDKGA). Targeted at the political domain, the approach enhances sentence scoring by leveraging manually curated domain keywords weighted by their contextual influence. These scores, combined with statistical features such as term frequency, sentence length, and position, guide a genetic algorithm to extract cohesive and informative sentence combinations for summary generation.

Kumar et al. [14] designed an extractive text summarization framework, which involves multiple text features including position, length, similarity, frequent words, and sentence numbers. These features are then combined with optimized weights, determined using Genetic Algorithm (GA), to rank sentences. Meena et al. [54] employed optimization based techniques like genetic algorithm. The effectiveness of genetic algorithms to determine optimal weights was exploited to discover the importance of features. Moreover, meta-heuristic/evolutionary approaches [51, 55] have been utilised in many similar works to choose the right sentences and determine the best weights for various text qualities that help in scoring the sentences. Jaya et al. [56] suggested employing genetic-case-based reasoning for the detection of cross-document theory structure (CST) leveraging five features: cosine similarity, word overlap, length type, noun phrase, and verb phrase. Furthermore, they introduced sentence scoring model using fuzzy reasoning. Wilson et al.[43] proposed a multi-document summarization (MDS) framework that compresses multiple documents into one using sentence similarity via Word Movers Distance (WMD) and Normalized Google Distance (NGD). It extracts syntactic (Longest Common Subsequence (LCS), n-gram, word order) and semantic (knowledge-based, sent2vec) features. Softmax Regression ranks sentence importance, and Spider Monkey Optimization selects the most relevant sentences for the final summary.

Potnurwar et al. [57] aimed a Binary Particle Swarm Optimization (BPSO)-based approach for multi-document extractive summarization, aimed at selecting an optimal subset of sentences that maximizes content coverage while minimizing redundancy. Each particle in the BPSO represents a binary string, where a value of '1' indicates the inclusion of a sentence in the summary. The optimization process is guided by a fitness function that incorporates multiple criteria, such as sentence relevance, inter-sentence similarity, and summary length constraints. The method ensures that selected sentences are both informative and non-redundant, effectively handling the complexity of summarizing across multiple documents. Verma et al. [55] extracted the significant sentences from each cluster which are recognized by their adjusted text feature scores, such as, sentence length, sentence position, name entity, numerical information, etc., In the second step, the teaching-learning based optimization approach is used to find the optimal summary. Gmez et al. [58] addressed the query-focused sentiment-oriented extractive multi-document text summarization problem involving multiple optimization criteria, including but not limited to, query relevance, redundancy reduction, and sentiment relevance. Al et al. [59] suggested a PSO method to solve the same problem. To choose the best summary of a document, the suggested method integrated informative scoring with semantic scoring using hand craft features to calculate the objective function in an unsupervised manner.

4) Machine learning-based approaches: Several research studies have employed these techniques for automatic summarization. Desai et al. [60] developed a supervised machine learning-based approach for automatic extractive summarization of Hindi text. The method involves selecting significant sentences by training classifiers-such as Naïve Bayes, Decision Trees, and Support Vector Machines (SVMs)-on a set of linguistic and statistical features including sentence position, term frequency, cue words, and sentence length. Gupta et al. [61] proposed an extractive summarization approach that leverages a diverse set of linguistic features to identify salient sentences. The method combines statistical, syntactic, and semantic features-including TF-IDF, sentence position, cue words, named entity presence, POS tags, and semantic similarity-to score and rank sentences for inclusion in the summary. A weighted scoring mechanism or a machine learning models (Naïve Bayes, Support Vector Machine, Random Forest, Decision Tree, Logistic Regression) is used to evaluate sentence importance based on the extracted features. The approach aims to improve the informativeness and coherence of summaries by capturing deeper linguistic characteristics of the text.

Kumari et al. [28] employed an unsupervised extractive summarization method tailored for Indian languages, utilizing clustering techniques to identify representative sentences from a document. The approach involves preprocessing the text (tokenization, stopword removal, stemming), followed by feature extraction using TF-IDF or semantic similarity measures. Sentences are represented in a high-dimensional feature space and grouped into clusters based on content similarity using algorithms such as K-means or hierarchical clustering. From each cluster, the most central or representative sentence is selected to form the final summary, ensuring content coverage and diversity. Mao et al. [62] proposed three hybrid extractive summarization methods that integrate supervised and unsupervised learning to enhance sentence importance scoring. Their methods aim to combine statistical sentence features with inter-sentence relationships to improve summary quality. The first method linearly combines sentence scores from both supervised classifiers and graph-based models. The second incorporates LexRank scores as an additional feature in the supervised model. The third introduces a novel biased-LexRank, using supervised scores as prior probabilities in a modified PageRank framework. Traditional machine learning (ML) involves supervised machine learning [63] classifiers to train the model by using human crafted features for classifying sentences as belonging to a summary (labeled as 1) or not belonging to a summary (labeled as 0) modelled as a binary classification problem. Classical machine learning (ML) techniques train supervised learning algorithms using relevant features that are manually selected [13] to generate summaries. Supervised machine learning approaches primarily work in two ways. In the first, hand-crafted features, such as sentence's length, sentence's position, cue-phrases words, thematic words, and uppercase words are fed to classical ML models such as

Naive Bayes [64–66], Decision Trees [64], DistAI [64], and support vector machines (SVM) [63, 66].

The model is then applied to categorise sentences in order to decide whether or not to include them in a summary. In order to create an extractive summarizer, Demiros et al. [67] directly extracted statistical and linguistic information from the original textual source. Machine learning-based extractive models, such as BERT-Sum [68], fine-tune pre-trained transformers for sentence-level extractive scoring, demonstrating strong performance over traditional techniques. Roul et al. [69] proposed an extractive multi-document summarization approach that integrates topic modeling with classification techniques to generate coherent and informative summaries. The method first uses a heuristic based on LDA and divergence measures to determine the optimal number of topics, then reduces the sentence pool in stages to retain only the most relevant content. Each sentence is scored using ten linguistic and semantic features (e.g., TF-IDF, Word2Vec, LDA2Vec), and machine learning classifiers-particularly Linear SVM-are employed to identify key sentences. Finally, one representative sentence per topic is selected based on combined local (silhouette) and global feature scores, and these are arranged by topic importance to form the final summary. Anand et al.[70] investigated the application of two neural network architectures for the task: Feedforward neural networks and convolutional neural networks combined with long short-term memory architectures. These models utilize word and sentence embeddings to capture semantic relationships, enabling effective summarization. Rezaei et al. [71] proposed a multi-step approach to sentence scoring, utilizing two separate neural networks: deep belief network and autoencoder neural network. Each network scored sentences in a document, enabling the identification of salient sentences for summarization.

Joshi et al. [48] introduced DeepSumm, a summarization approach that leverages a weighted combination of four key scores: Sentence content score, topic score, novelty score, and position score. By combining these scores, DeepSumm effectively identifies the most important sentences in a document, generating a comprehensive summary. Joshi et al. [72] proposed an approach that generates a summary by leveraging three sentence selection metrics: (1) sentence content relevance: determined by a deep auto-encoder, which assesses the semantic meaning of sentences, (2) sentence novelty: calculated by measuring the similarity among sentences represented as embeddings in a distributed semantic space, capturing unique information, and (3) sentence position: considering the sentence's location in the document. By combining these metrics, the approach effectively identifies the most informative sentences, generating a concise and comprehensive summary. Jain et al. [73] introduced the Deep Clustering Enhanced Summarization (DCESumm) approach, which leverages both unsupervised and supervised techniques for effective summarization. DCESumm combines: Unsupervised k-means clustering-based document-level score enhancement and Supervised sentence-level summary relevance prediction using BERT-based MLP (Multi-Layer Perceptron). By integrating these techniques, DCESumm achieves improved summarization performance. In deep learning (DL), features are learned automatically using embedding techniques [74] (such as word2vec, GloVe, and fasttextă) and then fed to deep learning neural networks such Convolutional Neural Network (CNN) and Bi-GRU to classify the sentences.

Joshi et al. [72] employed an unsupervised extractive summarization framework that selects salient sentences using three metrics: content relevance, novelty, and position relevance. Sentence embeddings are generated using a fine-tuned skip-thoughts model, and a deep auto-encoder is employed to learn a latent representation of the document. The contribution of each sentence is assessed by measuring the change in this representation when the sentence is removed. Novelty is calculated using cosine similarity to penalize redundancy, while position relevance dynamically favors early sentences. The final summary is formed by ranking sentences based on a weighted combination of these scores. Joshi et al. [48] proposed the model "DeepSumm" to capture the structural and semantic aspects of the document by combining topic and language vector encodings. Cheng et al. [75] combines an attention-based content extractor based on sentence and word extraction that jointly scores and selects sentences to produce extractive summaries. Al-Sabahi et al. [76] employed a novel extractive summarization model that leverages a hierarchical self-attention mechanism to mirror the structure of documentswords forming sentences and sentences forming documents. The model uses bidirectional Long Short-Term Memory (LSTMs) and self-attention at both the word and sentence levels to generate enriched embeddings, which are then used to classify whether a sentence belongs to the summary. Abstract features such as content richness, salience, novelty, and positional information are learned jointly. Treating summarization as a binary classification task.

Feng et al. [77] introduced an extractive approach using attentive encoder-based summarization (AES) model that produces both global information and the inter-relationships among sentences within a document. Zhou et al. [78] proposes NEUSUM, an end-to-end neural architecture that jointly learns sentence scoring and selection for extractive summarization, addressing the limitations of traditional methods that treat these as separate steps. Unlike conventional approaches that first score sentences independently and then select top-ranked ones, NEUSUM scores each candidate sentence dynamically based on both its content and the set of already selected sentences, measuring its relative Recall-Oriented Understudy for Gisting Evaluation (ROUGE) F1 gain. Two variants of the framework are developed: NEUSUMRNN, which uses a hierarchical RNN-based encoder and extractor, and NEUSUMBERT, which employs a BERT-based encoder and a GRU-based extractor with layer normalization. The system is trained using a KL-divergence loss between the predicted and normalized ROUGE-gain-based target distributions, and training supervision is created through a greedy algorithm that approximates optimal extractive labels from abstractive references. Zheng et al. [79] introduced Position-Aware Centrality-based SUMmarization (PACSUM), an unsupervised extractive summarization method that enhances sentence centrality computation in graph-based models. Unlike traditional approaches like TextRank, PACSUM incorporates directed edges based on sentence position and uses fine-tuned BERT embeddings to capture richer sentence semantics.

Liu et al. [80] proposed an unsupervised extractive text summarization method using Distance-Augmented Sentence Graphs (DASG), which enhances traditional graph-based approaches by incorporating not only sentence similarity and order but also the relative distance between sentences. This allows for finer-grained modeling of sentence importance. The method is extended to multi-document summarization by connecting individual document graphs through proximity-based cross-document edges. Using BERT for sentence embeddings and centrality-based ranking, the model outperforms existing unsupervised methods and competes closely with strong supervised baselines on benchmark datasets like Cable News Network and The Daily Mail (CNN/DailyMail), New York Times (NYT), and Multi-News. Zhong et al. [81] created supervised extractive summarization method based on the fusion of several networks, such as LSTM pointer networks, that have been pre-trained with BERT. Zhang et al. [82] employed HIBERT, a novel hierarchical bidirectional transformer encoder pre-trained on unlabeled data for extractive document summarization. HIBERT consists of two nested transformer layers: a sentence-level encoder and a document-level encoder. Unlike prior models that rely on noisy, heuristically generated sentence labels, HIBERT is pre-trained using a masked sentence prediction task, simulating a cloze-style objective at the sentence level. The model predicts missing sentences in a document using both preceding and succeeding context, making it well-suited for summarization. Xu et al. [83] proposed Semantic-aware Topic-based Abstract Summarization (STAS), an unsupervised extractive summarization framework that uses hierarchical transformers pre-trained on unlabeled data. It introduces two novel pre-training objectives: Masked Sentence Prediction (MSP) and Sentence Shuffling (SS), designed to learn sentence-level dependencies and coherence without human-labeled summaries. Once pre-trained, STAS selects summary-worthy sentences using a scoring mechanism based on attention weights and reconstruction loss.

Zhong et al. [84] introduce a model for solving the semantic text matching problem, where a source document and candidate summaries are matched in a semantic space. Wan et al. [85] applied a unified rank approach to score sentences, incorporating mutual influences between the two tasks into a graph model for both single and multi-document summarization. Gambhir et al. [74] proposed WL-AttenSumm, a deep learning-based extractive summarization model that uses a word-level attention mechanism combined with a Convolutional Bi-GRU (Bidirectional Gated Recurrent Unit) architecture. The model captures both syntactic and semantic relationships in text to select the most important sentences for summarization. It leverages pre-trained word embeddings (Word2Vec, GloVe, FastText). Muthu et al. [86] proposed a framework that utilizes a deep learning modifier neural network classifier, which leverages selected statistical features optimized by an improved fruit fly optimization algorithm. This approach combines the strengths of deep learning and evolutionary optimization to enhance the performance of the classifier. Zhu et al. [87] proposed an approach which is focused on incorporating extractive summarization methods within the neural sentence summarization framework.

However, we observed from this extractive literature that features such as incorrect words (e.g., spelling errors, informal contractions), which may reduce a sentences informativeness , and fluency score (e.g., Grammatical correctness, Syntactic cohesion), which may enhance sentence informativeness , graph-based feature like Node2Vec (it is used for semantic representations) , have not been explored for sentence scoring. The proposed features and scoring mechanisms are rarely validated or applied to low-resource Indian languages such as Hindi, Bengali, Tamil, or Telugu. This leads to a significant language bias and leaves a substantial gap in multilingual summarization research. In particular, the morphological complexity of many languages remains insufficiently explored and addressed. There is a noticeable gap in the use of regression-based machine learning models and supervised optimization models for ranking sentences by importance -an approach that holds promise for generating more nuanced and context-aware extractive summaries for low resource languages and standard language.

2.0.2 Abstractive Summarization

Abstractive summarization is the process of generating concise summaries in the models own words, capturing the key ideas of the original text, unlike extractive summarization which simply selects sentences. Existing works are done by researcher for abstractive summarization approach given below. A templatebased abstractive summarization method is done by Oya et al. [88] that used learned templates from human summaries to generate new summary sentences. It showed how templates and learned structures were used before neural approaches became dominant. Garg et al. [89] proposed a method called Key Extraction for Summarization of Tweets (KEST) for tweet summarization, which begins by constructing a word graph from the tweet corpus. They then applied a Markov Decision Process (MDP) to identify optimal chains of high-importance words. Finally, these keyphrases were combined to generate a coherent abstractive summary. A neural machine translation (NMT) system differs fundamentally from traditional machine translation methods. It represents a comprehensive and recently developed approach, as introduced by Kalchbrenner et al. [90]. NMT typically employs a unified neural network architecture most commonly an encoder-decoder framework-that jointly learns to translate input sequences. To enhance the performance of this basic encoder-decoder structure, Bahdanau et al. [91] proposed an attention mechanism that overcomes the limitations of fixed length input representations by allowing the model to dynamically focus on relevant parts of the source sentence during decoding. These techniques used the topic model as an additional mechanism to improve text generation. Nonetheless, these models have some sparseness issues and are difficult to train [92]. Current text summarization research focuses primarily on word embedding, which represents each element in some way [93], [94]. However, word embedding does not completely solve the polysemy problem. To address this issue, Embeddings from Language Models (ELMOs) [95] used bidirectional LSTM to train the language model, whereas hierarchical LSTM can grasp different levels of granularity information. Singh et al. [6] employed a sequence-to-sequence attention model based on recurrent neural networks (RNNs) for Indian English in ILSUM-2022, which has shown promising results for abstractive text summarization. Specifically, we used article text descriptions as input data in Bidirectional Long Short-Term Memory (Bi-LSTM) networks in the encoding layer, and generated a simplified summary of the article description as output using LSTMs in the decoding layer. Rush et al. [96] introduced a neural attention-based model for abstractive sentence summarization, laying the foundation for modern Seq2Seq architectures in summarization tasks. The proposed model combines a convolutional neural network (CNN) encoder with an attention-based feed-forward decoder, optimized for generating concise summaries of input sentences. Advancements in deep learning led to models like the Pointer-Generator Network [97], which combines copying and generation to improve factual accuracy. For this summarization approach, encoder decoder based RNN attention model on machine translation has been established by Ramesh Nallapatti et al. [15]. Word topic distribution of LDA has been combined to the sequence-to-sequence model to improve abstractive sentence [98]. They proposed a heuristic method that used the LDA techniques to identify the optimal number of independent topics.

Further improvements came with the introduction of transformer-based models, including Bidirectional and Auto-Regressive Transformers (BART) [99], T5 [100], and PEGASUS [101], which achieved state-of-the-art results on benchmark datasets. Tangsali et al. [102] employed fine-tuned PEGASUS model, which performed best for English and Gujarati, while the fine-tuned IndicBART model.

Agarwal et al. [103] employed the IndicBART multilingual sequence-to-sequence pre-trained model to generate text summaries for Indian languages. Taunk et al. [104] also explored the application of pre-trained models for abstractive summarization, specifically utilizing IndicBART and mT5 models. These models were fine-tuned for the summarization task, demonstrating their effectiveness in generating concise and informative summaries for Indian languages.

Moradi et al. [105] proposed clustering based framework by integrating powerful contextual embeddings from bidirectional encoder representations from transformers (BERT) and hierarchical clustering to enhance the extraction of meaningful content for document summarization. Agarwal et al. [103] employed the IndicBART model to generate text summaries on the provided Hindi dataset for ILSUM-2022. IndicBART is a multilingual sequence-to-sequence pre-trained model that supports 11 Indian languages. By leveraging the IndicBART model for training, they achieved a ROUGE-1 F-score of 0.544 on the testing dataset, demonstrating the model's effectiveness in generating high-quality summaries.

Chakraborty et al. [106] experimented pre-trained BART model, GPT model, and T5 model for English Languae in ILSUM-2022 at FIRE-2022. TeamMT-NLP-IIITH [9, 10] achieved the best performance across all three summarization tasks. The authors fine-tuned various transformer models, treating text summarization as a bottleneck task. Specifically: For Hindi and Gujarati, they fine-tuned MT5, MBart, and IndicBART for five epochs with a learning rate of 5e-5 and a maximum input length of 512. MT5 emerged as the best-performing model for Hindi, while MBart performed best for Gujarati. For English, they fine-tuned PEGASUS, BART, T5, and ProphetNet using similar hyperparameters, and PEGASUS outperformed the other models on text data. Satapara et al. [9] offers a comprehensive overview of the first edition of the ILSUM shared task, organized as part of the 14th FIRE-2022 conference. They covered the task's goals, approach, participant submissions, and evaluation outcomes, providing a valuable snapshot of the current research landscape in Indian language summarization. TeamBITSPilani [11] fine-tuned mT5 (mT5-multilingual-XLSum) model on the ILSUM dataset for all four languages. TeamNITK-AI [11] outperformed other teams where they fine-tuned T5-base on ILSUM English dataset. TeamIrlab-IITBHU [11] utilized name entity-aware text summarization, NER emerges as important factor to extract in-depth information and prioritising key entities for the summary by utilizing a pre-trained Muril-based Hindi NER model and fine-tuning MBART-50 for Hindi language. This literature is primarily based on the FIRE-2023 (ILSUM) shared task. The NITK-AI (SCALAR) team [107] utilized the T5-Base model for Indian English, achieving scores of 0.3321, 0.1731, 0.121, and 0.282 for ROUGE-1 F1, ROUGE-2 F1, ROUGE-4 F1, and ROUGE-L F1, respectively. The authors [108] employed mT5-base along with a fine-tuned T5-base to generate more accurate summaries, resulting in scores of 0.3022, 0.1111, 0.2504, and 0.8616 for English, and 0.2701, 0.1214, 0.2237, and 0.6782 for Hindi across the same metrics. The Irlab-IITBHU team [11] fine-tuned the MBART-50 pre-trained model, achieving ROUGE scores of 0.5625, 0.471, 0.4032, and 0.5373 for Hindi. Meanwhile, the BITS Pilani [11] team fine-tuned the mT5 (mT5-multilingual-XLSum) model, with results of 0.174, 0.0747, 0.0333, and 0.1655 for Gujarati, and 0.12, 0.0567, 0.0254, and 0.1087 for Bengali [11], respectively. Among all the teams,

NITK-AI [11] performed the best, fine-tuning the T5-base model on the ILSUM English dataset and achieving the scores mentioned. Recent developments in large language models (LLMs) such as GPT-3 [109], GPT-3.5 [110], Mistral-7B-Instruct-v0.2 [110], and GPT-4 [110] have shown remarkable capabilities in zero-shot and few-shot for abstyractive summarization. Borhan et al. [111] Compared different prompting styles (zeroshot, fewshot, rolebased) for summarization with GPT3.5 and LLaMA, providing evidence that prompt design significantly affects performance. Borhan et al. [112] evaluated how models like GPT3.5, ChatGPT, and GPT4 perform zeroshot crosslingual summarization. It shows that GPT4 achieves competitive results even without finetuning, using various prompt strategies.

Here, we observed from this abstractive summarization literature that the existing abstractive models fail for Indian English. The prior research-including sequence-to-sequence models with encoder-decoder architectures, pre-trained transformer models, and LLMs-was primarily conducted on standard English datasets, not on Indian languages. Indian languages are involved code-mixing, polysemy and morphological term, non-standard syntax, spelling variations, and culturally grounded expressionsthat cause current models to perform poorly.

2.1 Evaluation metrics

The performance of the proposed models for the text summarization task is assessed using two evaluation metrics: ROUGE [113] and BERTScore [114], focusing on Precision, Recall, and F_1-score.
ROUGE is a lexical, surface-level evaluation metric that compares the generated summary with the reference summary based on exact word matches. It measures similarity through n-gram overlap, with common variants including ROUGE-N (e.g., ROUGE-1, ROUGE-2) and ROUGE-L, which captures the longest common subsequence. However, ROUGE is highly sensitive to word order and spelling, making it best suited for evaluating extractive summaries, where maintaining the original wording is important.

ROUGE-N evaluates the overlap of n-grams between a candidate summary and a reference summary.

- match_n be the number of overlapping n-grams between the candidate and the reference
- $\text{total}_n^{\text{ref}}$ be the total number of n-grams in the reference summary
- $\text{total}_n^{\text{cand}}$ be the total number of n-grams in the candidate summary

Then, Recall, Precision, and F1-score for ROUGE-N metric are computed using Equation 2.1, 2.2, and 2.3:

$$\text{ROUGE-N}_{\text{Recall}} = \frac{\text{match}_n}{\text{total}_n^{\text{ref}}} \tag{2.1}$$

$$\text{ROUGE-N}_{\text{Precision}} = \frac{\text{match}_n}{\text{total}_n^{\text{cand}}} \tag{2.2}$$

$$\text{ROUGE-N}_{F_1} = \frac{2 \cdot \text{ROUGE-N}_{\text{Precision}} \cdot \text{ROUGE-N}_{\text{Recall}}}{\text{ROUGE-N}_{\text{Precision}} + \text{ROUGE-N}_{\text{Recall}}} \tag{2.3}$$

ROUGE-L is based on the Longest Common Subsequence (LCS) between the reference summary and the candidate summary.

- $LCS(R, C)$ be the length of the longest common subsequence between R and C
- R be the reference summary
- C be the candidate summary

Then, Recall, Precision, and F1-score for ROUGE-L metric are computed using Equation 2.4, 2.5, and 2.6:

$$\text{ROUGE-L}_{\text{recall}} = \frac{LCS(R, C)}{\text{length}(R)} \tag{2.4}$$

$$\text{ROUGE-L}_{\text{precision}} = \frac{LCS(R, C)}{\text{length}(C)} \tag{2.5}$$

$$\text{ROUGE-L}_{F_1} = \frac{(1 + \beta^2) \cdot \text{ROUGE-L}_{\text{recall}} \cdot \text{ROUGE-L}_{\text{precision}}}{\text{ROUGE-L}_{\text{recall}} + \beta^2 \cdot \text{ROUGE-L}_{\text{precision}}} \tag{2.6}$$

Where β is usually set to 1.

In contrast, BERTScore evaluates summaries at the semantic level, comparing the meaning of the generated text to the reference. It does this using contextual embeddings derived from BERT, enabling it to recognize paraphrased or reworded content with similar meaning. This makes BERTScore especially effective for assessing abstractive summaries, where preserving semantic similarity is more important than exact word matching. Let:
$C = \{c_1, c_2, ..., c_n\}$ represent the tokens in the candidate text,
$R = \{r_1, r_2, ..., r_m\}$ represent the tokens in the reference text,
and $\text{Emb}(t)$ be the contextual embedding of token t.

Then, Precision, Recall, and F1-score for BERTScore are defined in Equations 2.7, 2.8, and 2.9 respectively:
Precision: Each token in the candidate is compared to all tokens in the reference, and the highest similarity is used:

$$\text{Precision} = \frac{1}{n} \sum_{i=1}^{n} \max_{j} \text{cosine}(\text{Emb}(c_i), \text{Emb}(r_j)) \tag{2.7}$$

Recall: Each token in the reference is compared against all tokens in the candidate, again taking the highest similarity:

$$\text{Recall} = \frac{1}{m} \sum_{j=1}^{m} \max_{i} \text{cosine}(\text{Emb}(r_j), \text{Emb}(c_i)) \tag{2.8}$$

F1 Score: The F1 measure balances both precision and recall:

$$F_1 = \frac{2 \cdot \text{Precision} \cdot \text{Recall}}{\text{Precision} + \text{Recall}} \tag{2.9}$$

2.2 Datasets

This section presents twelve distinct datasets utilized to evaluate the proposed models. Among them, one dataset was introduced by Hermann et al. [115], and another by Over et al. [116], as shown in Table 2.1. Furthermore, three datasets were released by Satapara et al. [117] as part of the ILSUM shared task at FIRE-2022, which are listed in Table 2.2. In addition, seven more datasets were introduced under the ILSUM track at FIRE-2024, as shown in Table 2.3. A detailed description of each dataset is provided in the following subsections.

2.2.1 CNN\DailyMail & DUC-2002

The CNN/DailyMail[1] summarization dataset was compiled by researchers at Google DeepMind, led by Karl Moritz Hermann, and introduced in their 2015 paper titled "Teaching Machines to Read and Comprehend" [115]. The dataset comprises news articles collected from CNN (2007-2015) and the Daily Mail (2010-2015). CNN is an American television news channel known for its coverage of global and U.S. news, politics, business, health, and entertainment. In contrast, the Daily Mail is a British tabloid newspaper and online publication, primarily focused on news, entertainment, sports, and opinion. The dataset contains approximately 287,000 training, 13,000 validation, and 11,500 test instances. Each article averages around 800 words and is paired with 34 bullet-point highlights, which serve as abstractive summaries. While the original version was anonymized for reading comprehension tasks, later releases included non-anonymized summaries, making the dataset suitable for abstractive summarization research.

The DUC-2002 dataset is a benchmark corpus developed by the National Institute of Standards and Technology (NIST), with contributions from Paul Over and colleagues. It is part of the Document Understanding Conference (DUC) series and was designed to evaluate automatic text summarization systems, specifically targeting both single-document and multi-document summarization tasks. The DUC-2002 dataset is not publicly available for direct download. Researchers interested in accessing the data are required to contact NIST directly. Additional details are available on the official [DUC 2002 Guidelines page][2]. Over the years, this dataset has been widely adopted for both abstractive and extractive summarization research. It comprises 60 topic clusters, each containing approximately 10 news articles, along with one or more human-authored gold summaries per cluster. The details description of the each dataset can be seen in Table 2.1.

[1] `https://www.kaggle.com/datasets/gowrishankarp/newspaper-text-summarization-cnn-dai`
[2] `https://www-nlpir.nist.gov/projects/duc/guidelines/2002.html`

TABLE 2.1: Datasets description for CNN \DailyMail & DUC-2002.

Dataset	Summary length (in words)	Usage	No. Documents
CNN \ DailyMail	full length	Training	287,227
		Validation	13,368
		Testing	11,490
DUC_2002	100	Testing	567

2.2.2 Datasets for Indian Language

Automatic text summarization for Indian languages has received surprisingly limited attention from the NLP research community. While large-scale datasets exist for several languages-such as English, Chinese, French, German, and Spanish-no comparable, publicly available datasets exist for Indian languages. The few existing datasets are either not accessible to the public or are too small to be of practical use. To bridge this gap, the FIRE-2022 and FIRE-2024 (ILSUM) shared tasks have focused on developing reusable corpora specifically tailored for single-document summarization in Indian languages. Unlike summarization datasets in other languages, the ILSUM datasets present unique challenges, including code-mixing and script mixing. It is common for Indian news articles to incorporate English words and phrases even when the primary language of the article is not English. This linguistic characteristic makes the dataset especially challenging and uniquely reflective of the Indian multilingual context.

The ILSUM dataset sources articles from leading newspaper outlets and online news feeds in each language. This naturally yields a mix of genres such as: Politics, National & Regional News, Business & Economy, Entertainment & Culture, Sports Social Issues & General Affairs.

Including such genre labels strengthens dataset description and demonstrates coverage diversity.

2.2.2.1 Dataset-FIRE-2022 (ILSUM)

In its first edition of FIRE-2022 (ILSUM)[3], they covers two major Indian languages-Hindi and Gujarati-spoken by over 350 million and 50 million people respectively. In addition, the dataset includes Indian English, a widely recognized dialect that differs significantly from standard varieties of English spoken elsewhere. It is quite common for Indian news articles to incorporate English phrases, even when the main content is written in a regional language. The dataset for this task is constructed using article-headline pairs sourced from several leading Indian newspapers. Approximately 10,000 news articles are provided for each language. The objective is to generate a concise, fixed-length summary-either extractive or abstractive-for each article. The details description of the each dataset can be seen in Table 2.2 and the average number of sentences per article for each language is provided in parentheses.

TABLE 2.2: Dataset description for Hindi, English, and Gujrati language

Datasets	**Train data**	**Validation data**	**Test data**
English	12565 (21)	898 (21)	4487 (22)
Hindi	7957 (18)	569 (18)	2842 (18)
Gujarati	8457 (21)	605 (21)	3020 (20)

2.2.2.2 Dataset-FIRE-2024 (ILSUM)

The third edition of ILSUM [4] adds three Dravidian languages-Kannada, Tamil, and Telugu-in addition to Hindi, Gujarati, Bengali, and Indian English from the previous [118] edition. The dataset for this task is built using articles and headline pairs from several leading newspapers of the country. We provide over 15,000 news articles for each language (except Tamil). The task is to generate a meaningful fixed length summary, either extractive or abstractive, for each article. The details description of the each dataset can be seen in Table 2.3 and the average number of sentences per article for each language is provided in parentheses.

[3]https://ilsum.github.io/ilsum/2022/index.html
[4]https://fire.irsi.org.in/fire/2024/home

TABLE 2.3: Datasets description for multiple seven Indian language

Datasets	**Train data**	**Validation data**	**Test data**
English	9376 (26)	1500 (26)	2500 (26)
Hindi	10427 (24)	1500 (24)	3000 (23)
Gujarati	33630 (23)	-	1457 (23)
Telugu	9583 (26)	1065 (27)	4564 (27)
Kannada	10694 (26)	1188 (26)	5093 (26)
Tamil	4104 (18)	456 (17)	1955 (18)
Bengali	12356 (23)	-	2206 (21)

Chapter 3

Single Document Extractive Summarization Using Optimization Technique

The objectives of this chapter are following[1]:

- To introduce static particle swarm optimization and dynamic particle swarm optimization in supervised manner to generate extractive summaries.
- To clearly introduce and discuss two new features- "Incorrect word" and "Fluency Score" .
- To discuss the importance of each feature extracted for each sentence in the article.
- To compare the impact of static particle swarm optimization and dynamic particle swarm optimization in supervised manner.
- To examine the proposed model with error free and grammatically correct summaries indentification.

[1]The content of this chapter is based on [[7], (under revision)]

3.1 Introduction

Here are the some popular way to rank sentences over the years for summarization task, numerous features have been introduced, which can be grouped into four categories under the unsupervised approach: (i) word scoring, (ii) sentence scoring, (iii) graph scoring and (iv) word encoding representation using pre-trained embeddings (namely Word2Vec, GloVe and fastTest as done in [74]). Under the category of word scoring, prominent features are word frequency (WF) [23], use of the top n most frequent content words as thematic words, term frequency-inverse sentence frequency (TF-ISF) [23] [62], upper case [23], proper noun [23], word co-occurence [23] and lexical similarity [23], name entity (NE) [62] [55], and POS (noun, verb) [62]. (ii) A similar breadth of literature exists for features based on sentence scoring, where the prominent ones are cue-phrases [23], length of sentence (SL) [23] [62] [55], count of numerical data (ND) [23] [62] [55], position of sentence (SP) [62] [23] [55], sentence centrality (SC) [23] [55], and sentence resemblance to the title (ST) [23] [55]. Under the category of graph scoring (iii), features such as TextRank, markov random walk [62], busy path of a node, aggregation similarity [23] and , word form similarity (WFS) [119], word order similarity (WOS) [119], word semantic similarity (WSS) [119], and sentence similarity similarity measures (e.g., cosine similarity [48], jaccard similarity) [30, 38, 62, 120] [119] are some of the prominent ones. These features have been employed by various researchers for analysing single and multi-documents. Various scoring methods have been introduced in the literature using both classical machine learning (ML) [63–67] and deep learning (DL) techniques [48, 74, 75, 77]. These approaches leverage statistical, linguistic and semantic features in supervised manner to evaluate and extract the most relevant sentence segments.

Apart from machine learning and deep learning techniques, nature-inspired optimization algorithms have also been extensively explored for extractive text summarization. Al-Abdallah et al. [59] proposed extractive summarization approach for Arabic single-document. It used hybrid approach combining statistical features (e.g., title similarity, sentence length, sentence location, TF-IDF) and semantic similarity (using cosine similarity). A Directed Acyclic Graph is built to represent semantic relations, and applied PSO to select the most informative and semantically relevant sentences. Similarly, Jain et al. [121] used PSO to assign optimal weights to seven sentence-level features for generating summaries in the Punjabi language. Meena et al. [54] introduced a genetic algorithm that utilized 21 features (e.g., sentence position, cue words, title similarity, proper nouns, named entities) with trained weights to extract the optimal summary. Verma et al. [55] employed a hybrid extractive summarization model combining clustering, fuzzy inference, and Teaching Learning Based Optimization (TLBO) for scoring and selecting sentences. It uses a linear combination of Word Movers Distance and Normalized Google Distance to cluster sentences, with Gap statistics determining the optimal number of clusters. Sentence scores are computed using seven textual features (length, position, named entities, numeric, centrality, title word overlap, frequent words) and refined using fuzzy logic with human-generated rules. The model supports both single and multi-document summarization. Debnath et al. [50] used a Modified Binary Cat Swarm Optimization (MBCSO) approach for extractive single-document summarization, optimizing sentence selection based on content coverage, informativeness, and anti-redundancy. Each sentence is represented using seven features as mention in the scoring techniques (e.g., Sentence length, TF-IDF scores for unigrams, bigrams, trigrams, title similarity using Cosine and Word Mover Distance (WMD), Redundancy scores), with feature scaling applied for balanced scoring. Tanfouri et al. [42] presented an extractive Arabic text summarization system using Genetic Algorithms (GA). Sentences are scored by sum of frequencies of its words and selected based on a fitness function balancing informativeness (SentenceăScore) and redundancy (JaccardăSimilarity). The GA applies selection (Tournament (father) + Roulette wheel (mother)), crossover (One-point), and mutation (Bit-flip) to evolve optimal summaries. Saini et al. [51] proposed three novel extractive single-document summarization techniques-ESDS_SMODE, ESDS_MGWO, and ESDS_MWCA-based on multi-objective optimization using differential evolution, grey wolf optimizer, and water cycle algorithm, respectively. It employs sentence clustering guided by semantic similarity (via Word2Vec and Word Mover's Distance) and optimizes cluster validity indices (PBM and Xie-Beni) to select representative sentences. The framework automatically determines the number of clusters and ranks sentences using length, position, title similarity, and redundancy reduction.

Upon reviewing existing literature, it has been observed that prior studies have not introduced or utilized certain critical features-specifically, the incorrect word count and fluency score-in the context of extractive text summarization. Moreover,

Particle Swarm Optimization (PSO) has not yet been employed in a supervised manner to initialize the relative weights of these features for summary generation. Instead, earlier approaches have primarily applied PSO in a binary format, where it functions as a feature selection mechanism for identifying subsets of sentences to include in the summary. This binary representation focuses solely on whether a sentence should be included or excluded, without optimizing the individual feature contributions based on their relevance or quality.The absence of supervised weight initialization, as well as the omission of incorrect word and fluency-related features in prior work, highlights a significant research gap that this study aims to address.

This chapter proposes a new method, building on earlier studies, to effectively identify error-free and grammatically correct optimal summaries from single document. Two approaches have been proposed named XSumm-PSO and XSumm-DPSO to identify error-free and grammatically correct optimal summaries from the corpus.

The first approach proposes a PSO-based approach, called XSumm-PSO , that works well in a supervised learning manner to generate extractive summaries. Along with the nine existing hand-crafted features, namely, Sentence Length , Sentence Position , Numeric Data , Thematic Words and Aggregation Score , Name Entity, POS (noun and verb), and Entropy, a new feature based on the count of **"Incorrect word"** is fed as input to the XSumm-PSO algorithm. XSumm-PSO is a supervised particle swarm optimization method designed to optimize the weights of individual features using gold standard summaries as reference. These optimized weights are then utilized to rank sentences within a document for extractive summaries. The proposed models have been validated for three datasets: (i) DUC-2002, (ii) CNN/DailyMaily, and (iii) ILSUM-2022 (English), comprehensive dataset information is reported in Tables 2.1 and 2.2. The detailed description of the proposed model is mentioned under the Section 3.2.

The second approach proposed to extend our previous work by add on three elements: (1) apply dynamic PSO, (2) newly proposed **"Fluency Score"** feature (3) Enhanced the eights features named: Busy Path , TextRank , Lexical Similarity, Word Co-occurrence , Cue Words , Title Match , Upper Case , Term Weight. This approach present XSumm-DPSO , a supervised dynamic particle swarm optimization approach aimed at effectively optimizing the weights of individual features. By utilizing gold standard summaries, the method improves the accuracy of feature weight assignment. These optimized weights are then used to rank sentences within a document for extractive summaries. The proposed models have been validated for two datasets: (i) DUC-2002 and (ii) CNN/DailyMaily, comprehensive dataset information is reported in Table 2.1. The detailed description of the proposed model is mentioned under the Section 3.3.

3.2 Enhance the extractive summarization approach by initializing the relative weights of each feature using supervised PSO

The contributions of this paper are as follows:

(1) A supervised particle swarm optimization approach called XSumm-PSO is proposed that optimizes the weights assigned to each feature. The supervised approach uses the gold standard summaries to better optimize feature weights. The optimized weighted features are then used to rank the sentences in a document. To the best of our knowledge, this is the first time that a PSO-based approach has been used in a supervised manner for ETS. (2) A new feature "Incorrect word" is introduced that captures misspelled words in a sentence. It is used along with the existing nine features known in literature. (3) As a result of the proposed supervised PSO approach and "Incorrect word" feature, XSumm-PSO produces improvements of +2.7%, +0.8%, and +0.8% for ROUGE-1, ROUGE-2, and ROUGE-L scores, respectively, over state-of-the-art ETS methods on DUC (Document Understanding Conference) 2002 dataset. The corresponding improvements on CNN/DailyMail are +0.97%, +0.25%, and +0.49%. (4) The proposed approach was found to be statistically consistent across various runs when validated through t-test.

The remainder of this approach is organized as follows: Sub-section 3.2.1 elaborates on the proposed methodology; Sub-section 3.2.2 presents the state-of-the-art comparison; Sub-section 3.2.3 discusses the controlling parameters and results; Sub-section 3.2.4 presents the one-sample t-test; and Sub-section 3.2.5 provides the conclusion.

3.2.1 Proposed methodology

3.2.1.1 Problem statement

The goal of the extractive summarization task is to extract the ranked set of top-L most significant sentences from the document to represent the summary of the document. The resulting summary consists of L sentences. Let each document D be represented as a sequence of sentences, $(S_1, S_2, S_3, ...S_N)$, where $1 <= j <= N$. Each jth sentence is represented by a 10-dimensional feature vector $f_j = (f_j^1, f_j^2, f_j^3....., f_j^{10})$. In order to assign a feature weight to each feature score, the XSumm-PSO algorithm is proposed. The feature weights are represented as $w = (w_1, w_2, w_3....., w_{10})$. Then, the score of a sentence S_j is calculated as $w_j^1 * f_j^1 + w_j^2 * f_j^2 +, ... + w_j^{10} * f_j^{10}$. Finally, the sentences are sorted based on decreasing order of their scores such that S_j scores better than S_{j+1}. The rank of each sentence contributes to generate a good and meaningful summary of the document.

The Flow diagram of proposed method is shown in Figure 3.1. It has five main stages: (i) preprocessing, (ii) feature extraction, (iii) feature weight estimation by applying XSumm-PSO algorithm, (iv) sentence score and ranking, and (v) extractive summary generation. Each stage is described below.

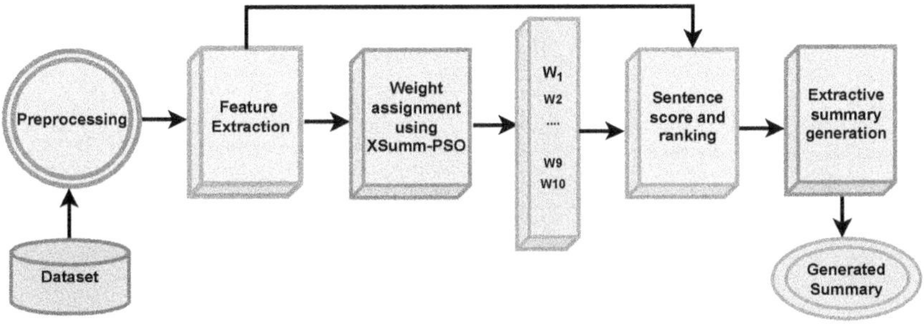

FIGURE 3.1: Flow diagram of the XSumm-PSO method

3.2.1.2 Pre-processing stage

Preprocessing eliminates the discrepancies in data and makes the data more structured and usable. It consists of the following sub-steps:

1. **Sentence segmentation:** Here, the text of a document is split into its constituent sentences. The split has been done using boundary constraints, such as, a full-stop or question mark.

2. **Word tokenisation:** This step tokenizes input sentences to words.

   We separate a text block into distinct words using a space delimiter.

3. **Stop-word removal:** This step removes stop words from the input text as per the stopwords list of natural language tool kit (NLTK) [2] library.

4. **Stemming:** Stemming removes prefixes, suffixes, and other affixes from words to reduce them to their basic form. Porter Stemmer, part of standard NLTK toolkit[3] was used for this purpose.

5. **Part of speech tagging (POS):** *pos_tag*[4] was used for POS tagging. The POS tags are used for feature extraction from the text.

6. **Name entity recognition (NER):** Here, NLTK pipeline toolkit[5] was used for NER Like POS tags, the NER tags are also used for feature extraction in the downstream framework.

Each pre-processed document is used for feature extraction in the next stage.

3.2.1.3 Feature extraction

For each pre-processed document, ten features are extracted for every sentence, which are described next. For convenience of notation, each feature is subscripted with ij indexing denoting the jth sentence in the ith document. A combined feature set for the jth sentence in the ith document is represented by a 10-d vector $f_{ij} = \{f_{ij}^1, f_{ij}^2, \ldots, f_{ij}^{10}\}$.

Each of the ten features used in this work and described next, is also computed on the following text for demonstration and better understanding using Figure 3.2:

[2]https://www.geeksforgeeks.org/removing-stop-words-nltk-python/
[3]https://www.guru99.com/stemming-lemmatization-python-nltk.html
[4]https://www.guru99.com/pos-tagging-chunking-nltk.html
[5]https://spacy.io/usage/processing-pipelines

I don't often dream at night and don't like having dreams beacuse usually my dreams are bad. Sometimes I even have nightmaressss. And it means that something is disturbing me mentally. While being younger I didn't have bad dreams so often, but now I see that it's some kind of a pattern for me.

FIGURE 3.2: Sample text. The words underlined in red indicate misspelled words.

1. **Sentence Length :(SL_{ij})**

   While very short sentences tend to be less informative, very long sentences tend to contain a lot of useless information. Hence, moderately long sentences are best placed. To encourage such sentences, the 'Sentence Length' feature captures how close the length of a sentence is to the average length of sentences in a given document. Specifically, it is computed as: (3.1), (3.2)

   $$SL_{ij} = 1 - \frac{|AvgL_i - L_j|}{maxL_i} \tag{3.1}$$

   where,
   $maxL_i$ denotes the maximum length of a sentence in the ith document,
   L_j denotes the length of the jth sentence, and
   $AvgL_i$ captures the average length of sentences in the ith document and is defined as

   $$AvgL_i = \frac{maxL_i + minL_i}{2} \tag{3.2}$$

   where,
   $minL_i$ denotes the minimum length of a sentence in the ith document. This feature value for the four sentences of the sample text in Figure 3.2 are =[0.67, 0.67, 0.78, 0.78].

2. **Sentence Position (SP_{ij}):** It has been observed [23] that a document's opening and closing sentences carry more important information than the sentences in the middle of the document. The "Sentence Position" feature captures this importance of the position of a sentence in a document in terms of how close the sentence is to the either end of the document. It is computed by Equation. 3.3

$$SP_{ij} = \frac{|\frac{N_i}{2} - j|}{\frac{N_i}{2}} \tag{3.3}$$

where, N_i denotes the number of sentences in the ith document. This feature value for the four sentences of the sample text in Figure 3.2 are are =[0.5, 0.0, 0.5, 1.0].

3. **Numeric Data (ND_{ij}):** Numerical values in a sentence are likely indicators of crucial details like date, money, and the quantity of damage,ăwhich in turn increase the importance of the sentence towards being included in the document summary. Let sentences be modelled through n-grams. Then, the value of numerical data feature for a sentence is the number of n-grams in the sentence having numbers. This feature value for the four sentences of the sample text in Figure 3.2 are are =[0, 0, 0, 0].

4. **Thematic Words (TW_{ij}):** Thematic words occur frequently in a document and capture the theme of the document. The presence of a thematic word in a sentence likely increases its importance towards the document summary. The thematic words feature captures the presence of thematic words in a sentence. We define the set of thematic words as the set of 50 most frequent words in a document. Let twc_{ij} denote the number of thematic words in the jth sentence. Let $twcMax_i$ denote the maximum number of thematic words in a sentence in the ith document. Then, the thematic words feature is defined as: (3.4)

$$TW_{ij} = \frac{twc_{ij}}{twcMax_i} \tag{3.4}$$

This feature value for the four sentences of the sample text in Figure 3.2 are = [0.8, 0.4, 0.4, 1.0].

5. **TF-ISF ($TF\text{-}ISF_{ij}$):** This feature is inspired by the popular TF-IDF (term frequency-inverse document frequency) [23] score of a word. Both TF-IDF and TF-ISF (term frequency-inverse sentence frequency) compute term frequency (TF) value in the same way. For the inverse frequency part (IDF or ISF), while the IDF is computed at the document level, ISF is computed at the sentence level. Specifically, ISF for a term t in the jth sentence of the ith

document, denoted $ISF_{ij}(t)$, is computed as:

$$ISF_{ij}(t) = log(\frac{N_i}{sf_i(t)}) \tag{3.5}$$

where,
N_i is the number of sentences in the ith document, and
$sf_i(t)$ is the fraction of sentences in the ith document containing the term t.

Thus, TF-ISF for the term t in the jth sentence of the ith document, denoted $TF\text{-}ISF_{ij}(t)$, is computed as:

$$TF\text{-}ISF_{ij}(t) = TF_i(t) * ISF_{ij}(t) \tag{3.6}$$

where, $TF_i(t)$ denotes the term-frequency of the term t in the ith document.

Further, the TF-ISF of the jth sentence of the ith document, denoted $TF\text{-}ISF_{ij}$, is computed as the sum of TF-ISF values of its constituent words. That is,

$$TF\text{-}ISF_{ij} = \sum_t TF\text{-}ISF_{ij}(t) \tag{3.7}$$

where, the summation is carried over all the terms in the jth sentence of the ith document.

$TF\text{-}ISF_{ij}$ is the final output that is used as a feature. This feature value for the four sentences of the sample text in Figure 3.2 are =[1.0, 0.76, 0.76, 1.0].

6. **Aggregation Score (AS_{ij}):** This feature captures the similarity of a sentence with respect to the remaining sentences in the document. For the ith document, let V_i denote its vocabulary. Then, the jth sentence in the ith document is represented as a vector of size $|V_i|$ having an entry corresponding to each term $t \in V_i$. For a term $t \in V_i$, the corresponding entry in the document vector is the TF-ISF value for t computed as per Equation. 3.6. The similarity between two sentences is computed as the cosine similarity between their corresponding vectors. The aggregation score (AS_{ij}) feature value for the jth sentence in the ith document is defined as the aggregation (sum) of the similarity scores of the sentence computed with the remaining sentences in the document. This feature value for the four sentences of the sample text in Figure 3.2 are =[1.0, 0.43, 0.57, 1.0].

7. **Name Entity (NE_{ij}):** Named entities (people, things, places, times, groups of people, etc.) are likely important constituents for summarizing a document. The named entity feature value of a sentence in a document is defined as the number of named entities in the sentence normalized by the maximum number of named entities in any sentence in the document. This feature value for the four sentences of the sample text in Figure 3.2 are =[0, 0, 0, 0].

8. **Part of Speech (NV_{ij}):** Nouns and verbs (parts of speech) are vital parts of a sentence that in turn affect its valuation towards being included in the document summary. This features captures the presence of nouns and verbs in a sentence. The part of speech feature value of a sentence in a document is defined as the number of nouns and verbs in the sentence normalized by the maximum number of nouns and verbs in any sentence in the document. This feature value for the four sentences of the sample text in Figure 3.2 are = [1.0, 0.0, 0.75, 1.0].

9. **Entropy (EN_{ij}):** The intuition behind this feature is to measure the element of surprise in a word. In terms of entropy[6], the rare words are more uncertain or surprising (low probability) and require more information to represent them than the common words (high probability). Because of the higher element of surprise, such words tend to have greater significance in generating document summaries. In a scenario where the word "t" appears only once in a document, the entropy is minimum, or equal to 0. If "t" is not an appropriate feature to represent the documents, that is, if "t" occurs in all the documents with the same frequency, then the entropy is maximum and equals 1. It is computed as:

$$EN_{ij} = \sum_{t \in T}^{j} -(p(t) * log_2(p(t))) \tag{3.8}$$

   where, ij denotes the jth sentence in the ith document, while $p(t)$ denotes the probability of a word in the document. T stands for the collection of words in the sentence. This feature value for the four sentences of the sample text in Figure 3.2 are = [1.0, 0.43, 0.57, 1.0].

10. **Incorrect Word(IW_{ij}):** We refer the misspelled or typographical errors in a sentence as 'Incorrect word'. We employed the SpellChecker (PySpellChecker

[6]https://medium.com/geekculture/how-to-calculate-the-entropy-of-an-entire-language-d17135b01282

TABLE 3.1: features description of each sentence in a document.

sentences	SL_{ij}	SP_{ij}	ND_{ij}	TW_{ij}	$TF-ISF_{ij}$	AS_{ij}	NE_{ij}	NV_{ij}	EN_{ij}	IW_{ij}
S_1	.67	.5	0	.8	1.0	1.0	0	1.0	1.0	-1
S_2	.67	0.0	0	.4	.76	.43	0	0.0	.43	-1
S_3	.78	.5	0	.4	.76	.57	0	.75	.57	0
S_4	.78	1.0	0	1.0	1.0	1.0	0	1.0	1.0	0

[7]) tool for identifying correct spellings. While incorrect words may exist in the original document, they are highly unlikely to be selected in the gold-standard human authored summaries. Hence, the presence of incorrect words in a sentence reduces its chance to be selected in the corresponding gold-standard human authored extractive summary of the document. Motivated by this, we introduce a feature called "Incorrect word" that captures the presence of incorrect words. It is defined as the negative of the number of misspelled words in the sentence normalized by the maximum number of misspelled words in any sentence in the document. To the best of our knowledge, this is the first time that such a feature has been used in deciding the importance of a sentence towards being included in the extractive summary of the document. This feature value for the four sentences of the sample text in Figure 3.2 are = [-1, -1, 0, 0].

For a comparative understanding, Table 3.1 shows the computed values of the ten used features for the sample text in Figure 3.2. These feature values are used by the XSumm-PSO optimization method (described next) that outputs weights denoting the relative importance of the above features. Using the sum of products of the relative weights and the corresponding feature values as the score of a sentence, the sentences are ranked in a document in order to generate the final extractive summary, which consists of the top L-ranked sentences.

3.2.1.4 XSumm-PSO

This section outlines the procedural steps for the proposed supervised Particle Swarm Optimization (PSO) method referred to as XSumm-PSO . A PSO approach consists of several components that work together to explore the solution space

[7]PySpellChecker is designed to detect misspelled words and provide correction suggestions based on word frequency statistics and edit-distance measures.

efficiently. The main components of PSO include: (1) initialization, (2) fitness function, (3) finding the current best solution, (4) update velocity and position of each particle, and (5) termination of algorithm. Each of these stages is described next; however, before explaining each stage, the objective function and some key points of the proposed XSumm-PSO are described.

a) Objective: Feature weight estimation: This section describes XSumm-PSO – a particle swarm optimization (PSO) [122] based technique for weight estimation of each feature. XSumm-PSO, depicted in Figure 3.3, behaves in a supervised manner during the training time because it uses the human generated target summaries to calculate fitness score of the objective function during optimization. Like PSO, XSumm-PSO is based on the idea of processes involving particle's position and velocity. The optimization process is divided into position and velocity phases, where the position phase is responsible to enhance the solutions from the velocity phase. XSumm-PSO searches in the local and global search spaces of the input document to find the relevant sentences and then determines a set of optimal feature weights. It is described in detail next.

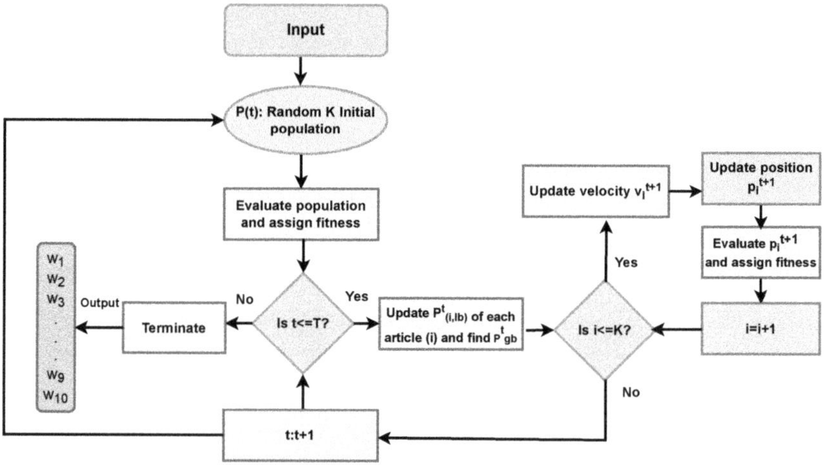

FIGURE 3.3: Working of the PSO method

b) The XSumm-PSO algorithm: In terms of PSO, here, a randomly initialized weight vector represents a particle and a solution. During an iteration, each vector is optimized on an associated document. In subsequent iterations, the associated set of documents keep changing. After multiple such iterations, it is expected that each weight vector has seen sufficient number and variety of documents to

TABLE 3.2: position vector description.

P_1	P_2	P_3	P_4	P_5	P_6	P_7	P_8	P_9	P_{10}
.66	.57	.12	.14	.67	.43	.23	.33	.45	.89

TABLE 3.3: velocity vector description.

V_1	V_2	V_3	V_4	V_5	V_6	V_7	V_8	V_9	V_{10}
.66	.55	.11	.44	.37	.43	.23	.84	.45	.77

represent a solution that will generalize well over the documents in the training set. During iterations, each solution moves around the search space with a velocity that is constantly changing in accordance with its own and its neighbour's past behaviour. Throughout the search process, the weight-vector prefers to move toward better locations represented by higher fitness scores.

Each individual solution in the population is a 10-dimensional vector corresponding to weights assigned to the above 10 features. The vector of velocity in Table 3.3 (randomly generated for illustration purpose) and the vector of position in Table 3.2 (randomly generated for illustration purpose) are attached to each document in the population. The fitness value of a solution weight vector is assessed as the ROGUE-1 recall score of the summary generated on the associated document. The ROGUE-1 recall score is computed with respect to the human generated summary of the associated document, where weight values are optimized by the algorithm during the course of training. Each solution has a speed that controls how far and in what direction in the search space the solution moves. Following the current optimal weight-vector solution, the particles move through the problem space. The proposed PSO approach consists of the following:

1. **Initialization:** Each weight vector's initial position and velocity are represented by a set of numbers generated at random in the range (0, 1). The number of particles in an iteration range from 1 to K, and the index of a solution particle is denoted by the notation i. The dimension index $d \in [1, D]$, where D denotes the number of dimensions. The position of the ith particle (i.e., a weight vector) is denoted by the symbol p_i, $p_i = [p_{i1}, p_{i2}, ..., p_{id}, ..., p_{iD}]$. p_{id} denotes the ith solution's value for the dth dimension. A document's velocity is denoted by the symbol $v_i = [v_{i1}, v_{i2}, ..., v_{id}, ..., v_{iD}]$. Each solution can be defined as $K_{i(s_j)} = K_{i(s_j)1}, K_{i(s_j)2}, K_{i(s_j)3}......K_{i(s_j)dim}$, where $dim = 10$ denotes the number of features of a document of the size of the weight vector.

The termination criteria, i.e., the number of iterations the optimization will run for, denoted T, is also initialized.

2. **Fitness function:** In this stage, the document contains listing the features of each sentence (similar to the one shown in Table 3.1). Each document is linked to a positional vector (similar to the one shown in Table 3.2). The positional vector is multiplied linearly with the respective features of the sentences in a document. The sentences are selected out of each document based on the weighted scores of their features. The top L sentences with the highest scores are selected for evaluation using the objective function described in Eqn. 3.9. A ROUGE-1 recall is used as the fitness function to obtain an accurate quantitative value. It determines whether the extracted sentences and the human-authored summaries are identical by using the overlapping words. To put it simply, “recall" (in the context of ROUGE-1) relates to how much of the human-authored summary is being recovered from the system-generated summary. It is computed as:

$$Recall = \frac{S\_G\_S \cap H\_A\_S}{H\_A\_S} \tag{3.9}$$

where, S_G_S and H_A_S represent the system generated and human-authored summaries, respectively. In this way, we are able to get K values for the objective function (one for every solution). The best solution globally is considered to be the one with the highest fitness value.

3. **Finding the current best solution:** First, personal best positions $p^t_{(i,lb)}$ and global best positions $p^t_{(gb)}$ are updated based on their current personal best position, which is the one having the highest fitness value.

   (a) **Update personal best position $p^t_{(i,lb)}$ of each solution:** $p^t_{(i,lb)}$ is the personal best position of the ith solution in the tth generation. To maximize the objective function, we update the personal best position $p^t_{(i,lb)}$ using the Eqn.(3.10).

$$p^{t+1}_{(i,lb)} = \begin{cases} p^{t+1}_i, & \text{if } f(p^{t+1}_i) < f(p^t_i) \\ p^t_i, & otherwise \end{cases} \tag{3.10}$$

   (b) **Update global best position $p^t_{(gb)}$ of each solution:** For finding the global best of the solutions, we need to first find the personal best position of each solution. Then, the solution having the personal best value corresponding to the highest fitness value is initialized as the global best position $p^t_{(gb)}$ in the tth generation. The global best position $p^t_{(gb)}$ is calculated using Eqn. 3.11.

$$p^t_{(gb)} \in \{p^t_i, ..., p^t_K\} | f(p^t_{(gb)}) = max\{f(p^t_i), ..., f(p^t_K)\} \tag{3.11}$$

where, K is the number of particles in the population.

4. **Update velocity and position of each particle:** First, velocity of a particle is updated and then its position is updated based on its updated velocity.

   (a) **Update velocity of each particle:-** For each feature value of each particle solution, its velocity is updated based on its current velocity as follows:

$$v^{t+1}_i = wv^t_i + c_1 r_1 (p^t_{(i,lb)} - p^t_i) + c_2 r_2 (p^t_{gb} - p^t_i) \tag{3.12}$$

   where,

   - wv^t_i is the momentum part. It has the knowledge of the previously flown routes. It also prevents the particle's direction from changing drastically because of the inertia component w,
   - Cognitive part $c_1 r_1 (p^t_{(i,lb)}$-$p^t_i)$: It evaluates performance in light of previous achievements. It has the knowledge of the previous best position,
   - Social part $c_2 r_2 (p^t_{gb} - p^t_i)$: It evaluates performance relative to the neighbours,
   - v_i = is the ith document's velocity,
   - $p^t_{(i,lb)}$ = the personal best position that has so far been discovered,
   - $g^t_{(gb)}$ = the global best position found from the document's neighbourhood, and
   - r_1 and r_2 are two uniformly chosen random numbers from [0, 1] and personal and social acceleration coefficients are c1 and c2, respectively.

(b) **Update position of each document:-** The position of a document, represented by the corresponding weight vector, is updated based on its current velocity and previous position.

$$p_i^{t+1} = p_i^t + v_i^{t+1} \tag{3.13}$$

where, p_i denotes the ith document's current location in the population.

5. **Termination of algorithm:** The above steps are followed in each iteration. The total number of iterations are defined by the user. The optimization algorithm terminates after running for these number of iterations. Then, the global best position vector is produced, which is further used for testing purpose. It is represented as $w_i = w_i^1, w_i^2, w_i^3, ...w_i^{10}$.

3.2.1.5 Sentence Score and Ranking

The score of each sentence in each article is computed as $w_i * f_{ij} = w_i^1 * f_{ij}^1 + w_i^2 * f_{ij}^2 +, ... + w_i^{10} * f_{ij}^{10}$. The sentences are then ranked based on their scores.

3.2.1.6 Extractive Summary Generation

Once the sentences are ranked, the top the C=30% of the articles are chosen to constitute the generated extractive summary.

TABLE 3.4: Controlling parameters setting.

Parameters	**Value**
Number of articles (K)	20
Maximum number of iteration (T)	1000
Number of dimensions (D)	10
Lower bound	0
Upper bound	1
Inertia weight(w)	.75
c1	1
c2	1

3.2.2 Baseline models

The ROUGE metric make it easier to compare our findings with those of other methods. The maximum length of the summaries for the DUC-2002 dataset goes till 100 words, while the summaries in the CNN/DailyMail and ILSUM-2022 can be of any length. The performance of our proposed model is compared with the following state-of-the-art methods. We categorize these state-of-the-art techniques into three categories based on the benchmarked datasets on which they were evaluated:

The following methods were used for comparison on both CNN/Daily-Mail and DUC datasets:

NN-SE [75] combines an attention-based content extractor based on sentence and word extraction with a hierarchical document encoder that jointly scores and selects sentences to produce extractive summaries.

SummaRuNNer [123] is an extractive summarizer based on simpleăRNN-based sequence classifier. It suggests a novel abstractive training mechanism that eliminates the necessity for extractive annotated data at the training time.

HSSAS [76] employ a hierarchical structured self-attention mechanism for generating sentence and document embeddings to serves as an additional source of information to guide summary extraction of the summarization task treated as a classification problem.

DeepSum [48] computes multiple types of scores. The score computed from the topic model is called Sentence Topic Score (STS), while the score generated through the word embeddings is referred to as Sentence Content Score (SCS). Additionally, introduce Sentence Novelty Score (SNS) and Sentence Position Score (SPS). Then conduct a weighted fusion of these four scores for each sentence in the document to calculate a Final Sentence Score (FSS).

Baseline model represents method without utilizing the proposed PSO approach. Following this paradigm, we have created two base models based on number of features. The name of baseline models are Baseline-9F and Baseline-10F. Baseline-9F method consists of nine features namely Sentence Length, Sentence Position, Numeric Data, Thematic Words, TF-ISF, Aggregation Score, Name Entity, Part of Speech, and Entropy. Another Baseline-10F method consists of existing nine features with newly "incorrect word" feature.

The following methods were used for comparison on the CNN/Daily-Mail dataset only:

Bi-AES [77] introduce an attentive encoder-based summarization (AES) model that produces a comprehensive document representation by taking into account both global information and the interrelationships among sentences within the document.

RNES [124] proposes a neural coherence model to obviate the need of feature engineering to capture the cross-sentence semantic and syntactic coherence patterns and can be trained using Reinforced Neural Extractive Summarization (RNES) model.

NeuSum [78] proposed a framework for end-to-end neural networks. Through a neural document encoder, the input document's sentences are represented as real-valued vectors. The method then generates the output summary by extracting each significant sentence individually.

PACSUM(BERT) [79] is a technique for unsupervised summarization that uses BERT to identify sentence similarity and builds directed edge networks to support the claim that any two nodes' contributions to their respective centrality are influenced by their positions in the document.

DASG [80] is a graph-based single-document unsupervised extraction approach that builds a distance-augmented sentence graph (DASG) from a document, allowing for fine-grained sentence modelling and characterising the original document structures.

JECS [125] consists of a sentence extraction model coupled with a compression classifier that determines whether or not to remove syntax-derived compression for each sentence.

HIBERT [82] is a pre-trained model trained with unlabeled data for document encoding. It solves the problem of hierarchical encoder and inaccurate labels of neural extractive summarization models.

PNBERT + RL [81] is a supervised extractive summarization method based on the fusion of several networks, such as LSTM pointer networks, that have been pre-trained with BERT and then further improved by reinforcement learning.

STAS +PACSUM [83] proposed unsupervised extractive summarization that extracts key sentences from a document without using labelled summaries for training. Transformer attentions can be used to rank sentences using sentence-level self attentions for unsupervised extractive summarization.

MATCHSUM [84] is an extractive summarization model work for solving the semantic text matching problem, where a source document and candidate summaries are matched in semantic space.

The following methods were used for comparison on the DUC 2002 dataset only:

URANK [85] applied a unified rank approach to score sentence rankings, incorporating mutual influences between the two tasks into a graph model for both single and multi-document contexts.

Tgraph system [41] presented a methodology based on a weighted graphical representation of documents derived from topic modelling. They simultaneously optimise significance, coherence, and non-redundancy using ILP.

Egraph [41] utilize a weighted graphical representation of documents derived from topic modeling and concurrently optimize importance, coherence, and non-redundancy through ILP (Integer Linear Programming).

CoRank [38] proposed a word-sentence co-ranking model that combines the relationship between words and sentences with an unsupervised graph-based ranking model.

SummCoder [72] generates a summary based on three sentence selection metrics, including relevance of sentence content, sentence novelty, and sentence position relevance using different methods

3.2.3 Controlling Parameters & Results

In this study, we discussed about the controlling parameters and results of proposed approach. These controlling parameters which is mention in the Table 3.4 is used to train the XSumm-PSO method. Further, we evaluated the performance of the proposed XSumm-PSO approach on three benchmark datasets using ROUGE-N (N =1,2) and ROUGE-L metrics and its details are mention under the section 2.1. The detailed description of the used datasets are mentioned in Table 2.1 and Table 2.2 under the sections 2.2.1 and 2.2.2.1, respectively. The results for the CNN/DailyMail, DUC 2002, and ILSUM-2022 (English language) datasets are presented in Table 3.5. These results are obtained with and without using the newly introduced "incorrect word" feature and after ten runs of XSumm-PSO algorithm with these parameters as given Table 3.4 on each dataset. The XSumm-PSO approach achieved ROUGE-1 scores of 55.9 (recall), 34.05 (precision), and 42.32 (F1-score), and ROUGE-L scores of 50.7 (recall), 19.72 (precision), and 28.29 (F1-score) on the DUC 2002 dataset. For the CNN/DailyMail dataset, the model produced ROUGE-1 scores of 45.38 (recall), 17.01 (precision), and 24.75 (F1-score), while the ROUGE-L scores were 41.04 (recall), 10.04 (precision), and 16.60 (F1-score). On the ILSUM-2022 dataset, it achieved ROUGE-1 scores of 66.62 (recall), 11.94 (precision), and 20.25 (F1-score), along with ROUGE-L scores of 58.22 (recall), 10.24 (precision), and 17.42 (F1-score). The results after comparing the proposed XSum-PSO model with the baseline models (described in Section 3.2.2) have been included in Tables 3.5, 3.8, and 3.9 for datasets ILSUM-2022, DUC-2002, and CNN/Dailymail, respectively. We present the summaries generated by our approach for randomly selected documents from the DUC 2002 and ILSUM-2022 datasets, as shown in Tables 3.6 and 3.7, respectively. This displays the generated summaries for both documents, with the "incorrect word excluded. The blue-highlighted text in the system-generated summaries aligns with the corresponding blue text in the reference summaries, indicating their similarity.

3.2.3.1 Discussion

From a theoretical and conceptual standpoint, three key factors contribute to the effectiveness of the proposed XSumm-PSO approach: (i) Supervised Use of PSO: The approach employs Particle Swarm Optimization in a supervised manner by leveraging gold-standard summaries during training. To the best of our knowledge, this is the first time such a supervised application of PSO has been explored in the literature. This enables the PSO algorithm to utilize information from the reference summaries to more effectively optimize feature weights, thereby enhancing sentence scoring. (ii) Weighted Feature Selection: Unlike existing methods that

TABLE 3.5: The results of proposed XSumm-PSO model on DUC 2002, CNN/DailyMail and FIRE-2023 (ILSUM) datasets.

Datasets	Approach	*R1_rec*	*R1_pre*	*R1_f1*	*Rl_rec*	*Rl_pre*	*Rl_f1*
CNN/DailyMail	XSumm-PSO-(Incorrect Word)	44.2	16.39	23.91	40.7	10.18	16.29
	XSumm-PSO	**45.38**	17.01	24.75	**41.04**	10.40	16.60
DUC-2002	XSumm-PSO-(Incorrect Word)	53.2	32.29	40.19	46.0	18.55	26.44
	XSumm-PSO	**55.9**	34.05	42.32	**50.0**	19.72	28.29
ILSUM-2022	Baseline-9F	35.26	17.21	23.16	27.91	13.55	18.24
	Baseline-10F	54.44	12.46	20.28	46.29	10.48	17.09
	XSumm-PSO-(Incorrect Word)	45.12	16.93	24.62	36.08	13.33	19.47
	XSumm-PSO	**66.62**	11.94	20.25	**58.22**	10.24	17.42

TABLE 3.6: XSumm-PSO generated summary and Gold summary for a document from DUC-2002 dataset.

XSumm-PSO
Thousands of miners in the Vorkuta region of the Soviet Union are expanding their strike and are blocking coal shipments. They are demanding the government fulfil promises to improve living and job conditions. "Officials said that the strikes could force fuel rationing during the Soviet Union's severe winter."**A regional court in Vorkuta ruled that the latest round of strikes is illegal, but did not impose any penalties.** Coal miners in Vorkuta and in Ukraine struck for two weeks in the summer, but returned to work in July after Parliament passed a resolution, promising reforms.
Gold summary
Coal miners in the northern region and the Ukraine struck for two weeks this summer but returned to work in July after parliament passed a resolution promising reforms, **including improved social and economic conditions.** Thousands of miners in the northern Vorkuta region are expanding their strike and some are blocking coal shipments, **the Soviet news media reported Friday.** Soviet officials have said the strikes could force fuel rationing during the Soviet Union's severe winter. The miners are demanding the government fulfil promises of improved living and job conditions.

either fully retain or discard features, our approach assigns a continuous weight to each feature. A higher weight indicates greater importance in the sentence scoring process. This mechanism allows the model to incorporate all features based on their individual contributions, ensuring that useful information is not discarded prematurely. (iii) Incorporation of the Incorrect word Feature: In addition to the nine existing hand-crafted features, we introduce a novel feature that captures the

TABLE 3.7: XSumm-PSO generated summary and Gold summary for a document from ILSUM-2022 dataset.

XSumm-PSO
Obama edges President Donald Trump, 17 per cent 14 per cent, former secretary state Clinton moved past Michelle Obama, 9 per cent 7 per cent First lady Melania Trump scored one per cent, poll said.
Gold summary
Obama edges **out** President Donald Trump, 17 per cent **to** 14 per cent, **while** former secretary **of** state Clinton moved past Michelle Obama, 9 per cent **to** 7 per cent **and** First lady Melania Trump scored one per cent, **the** poll said.

TABLE 3.8: Comarison analysis of proposed XSumm-PSO model with other state-of-the-art techniques on DUC 2002 dataset.

Method	ROUGE-1	ROUGE-2	ROUGE-L
NN-SE [75]	47.4	23.0	-
SummaRuNNer[123]	47.4	24.0	14.7
Egraph+coh [41]	47.9	23.8	-
Tgraph+coh [41]	48.1	24.3	-
URANK [85]	48.5	21.5	-
Summcoder [72]	51.7	27.5	44.6
HSSAS[76]	52.1	24.5	48.8
CoRank [38]	52.6	25.8	-
DeepSumm [48]	53.2	28.7	49.2
Baseline-9F	47.53	19.55	27.21
Baseline-10F	51.12	21.79	29.48
XSumm-PSO (-) "incorrect word"	**53.2**	**27.0**	**46.0**
XSumm-PSO	**55.9**	**29.5**	**50.0**

count of misspelled or incorrect words in a sentence. Through our observations, we found that sentences containing such errors are less likely to appear in high-quality summaries. This insight led to the creation of the Incorrect word feature, which penalizes sentences with spelling or grammatical mistakes, thereby lowering their chances of being selected in the final summary. Together, these components enhance the robustness and quality of the proposed summarization approach.

Our proposed approach centers on extractive text summarization, employing the XSumm-PSO method with and without the inclusion of the "Incorrect word" feature, across three datasets. The "Incorrect word" are removed from a document to improve the efficiency of the generated summary using XSumm-PSO approach. Another finding is that XSumm-PSO undergoes supervised training where the cost function is calculated using ROUGE-1(recall) and the human-authored summaries are utilized to calculate fitness score. ROUGE-1(recall) help to find the right path

TABLE 3.9: Comarison analysis of proposed XSumm-PSO model with other state-of-the-art techniques on CNN/DailyMail dataset.

Method	ROUGE-1	ROUGE-2	ROUGE-L
NN-SE [75]	35.5	14.7	32.2
Bi-AES[77]	38.8	12.6	33.85
SummaRuNNer [123]	39.6	16.2	35.3
PACSUM(BERT) [79]	40.7	17.8	36.9
RNES [124]	41.2	18.8	37.7
STAS+PACSUM [83]	41.26	18.18	37.48
NeuSum [78]	41.5	19.0	37.9
DASG [80]	41.6	18.5	37.8
JECS [125]	41.7	18.5	37.9
HSSAS [76]	42.3	17.8	37.6
HIBERT [82]	42.3	19.9	38.8
PNBERT+RL [81]	42.6	19.6	38.8
DeepSumm [48]	43.3	19	38.9
MATCHSUM (RoBERTa-base) [84]	44.41	20.86	40.55
Baseline-9F	40.47	17.88	34.74
Baseline-10F	42.06	18.11	39.07
XSumm-PSO (-) "incorrect word"	**44.2**	**20.7**	**40.7**
XSumm-PSO	**45.38**	**21.11**	**41.04**

of the particle towards finding the best fitness score utilizing the position vector and velocity vector. The fitness score is calculated by counting the number of match words between the system generated summary and the human-authored summary. We have also evaluated the produced results showcase the effectiveness of the proposed system compared to various state-of-the-art techniques as shown in Table 3.8 and Table 3.9 on two bechmark datasets DUC 2002 and CNN/Daily-Maily, respectively. For both datasets, our suggested method outperforms state-of-the-art RNN-based summarization techniques, including NN-SE, SummaRuNNer, SummCoder, and HSSAS, all of which make use of the document's latent topic information. Furthermore, readers perceive the summaries generated by the system as coherent and easily readable.

In this proposed method, we have used ten features to represent a sentence in the document. These features are based on statistical and linguistic methods and are independent of the language and the type of documents. So, we believe that these features and the proposed method will readily generalize to other languages and types of documents. Instead of feature selection as done in previous SOTA methods, here the proposed XSumm-PSO framework is trained by initializing the

10-dimensional populations for extractive text summarization. Here the values of population for each feature are normalized between 0 to 1. With the help of population values for each feature, the XSumm-PSO framework is trained to provide the relative weights of each feature, which are responsible for generating the summaries equivalent to the human generated target summaries.

XSumm-PSO has a low convergence rate in the iterative optimization process. The convergence rate in Particle Swarm Optimization (PSO) refers to how quickly the algorithm reaches a solution, particularly the optimal or near-optimal solution. Factors contributing to low convergence include Exploration-Exploitation Balance [126], Inertia Weight, Swarm Topology, Parameter Settings, Premature Convergence, Dynamic Environments [127], Initialization, and Fitness Landscape.

To address the issue of low convergence rates in PSO, researchers often experiment with different parameter settings, swarm typologies, and strategies to balance exploration and exploitation. Fine-tuning these aspects can enhance the algorithm's convergence speed and overall performance in finding optimal solutions.

When comparing the proposed XSum-PSO with other methods, the optimization method that is often compared with PSO is Genetic algorithms (GA). While GA involves the evolution of populations through genetic operations like crossover and mutation, PSO relies on particle movements. However, we used PSO because it typically requires less memory as it maintains a smaller population of solutions compared to GAs. It has also fewer parameters to fine-tuning.

XSumm-PSO uses hand crafted features that do not capture the semantic information. Working to overcome this has the possibility of improving the results further.

3.2.4 One sample t-test

The one-sample t-test is used to determine whether the mean of a sample significantly differs from a known or hypothesized population mean. The test statistic, denoted as t, is calculated using the following formulas:

$$t = \frac{\bar{x} - \mu_0}{S_{\bar{x}}} \tag{3.14}$$

$$\text{where} \quad S_{\bar{x}} = \frac{s}{\sqrt{n}} \tag{3.15}$$

Here, $\bar{x}$ represents the sample mean, μ_0 is the hypothesized population mean, s is the sample standard deviation, and n is the sample size. The standard error of the mean, $S_{\bar{x}}$, accounts for variability in the sample.
The calculated t-value is then compared against the critical t-value from the t-distribution table, based on the degrees of freedom (df = n-1) and the selected confidence level. If the computed t-value falls within the acceptance region (i.e., is less than the critical t-value), the null hypothesis is not rejected.

3.2.4.1 Test for consistency

Our proposed approach, XSumm-PSO, is inherently iterative and stochastic in nature. Consequently, we evaluated the consistency of its results across multiple runs. To verify the reliability of these outcomes, we performed a statistical t-test and formulated a hypothesis to assess their statistical significance.

- Null hypothesis H_0: The test result does not vary significantly accross various runs.
- Alternative hypothesis H_a: They vary significantly.

For performing t-test with confidence level of 5% [51, 128, 129], the null hypothesis claimsăno significantădifference across various runs. According to the alternative theory, substantial differences should exist. We have calculated the sample mean individually from 3 groups (group-1, group-2, group-3 contains the list of scores ROUGE-1, ROUGE-2, ROUGE-L, respectively) of our approach for each datasets and derived the conclusion for the population means. We have run XSumm-PSO approach for ten times on the three benchmark datasets. We found that the results do not vary significantly in each run; the average score is reported in Table 3.5 for CNN/DailyMail, DUC 2002, and ILSUM-2022 datasets.

For the CNN/DailyMail dataset, the computed t-statistical values were 1.072, 0.272, and 2.243 for ROUGE-1, ROUGE-2, and ROUGE-L, respectively. These values were then compared with the t-critical value of 2.35 at a significance level of $\alpha = 0.05$. Since all t-statistical values were below the t-critical threshold, we conclude that the null hypothesis cannot be rejected. This indicates that the test results do not vary significantly across different runs. Similar comparable results were observed for both the DUC-2002 and ILSUM-2022 datasets. Specifically, the t-statistical values for the DUC-2002 dataset were 0.120, 0.014, and 0.210 for ROUGE-1, ROUGE-2, and ROUGE-L, respectively. For the ILSUM-2022 dataset, the corresponding values were 0.059, 0.070, and 0.060. These values were compared against the t-critical value of 2.35 at a significance level of $\alpha = 0.05$. In all cases, the t-statistical values were lower than the critical threshold, indicating that the null hypothesis could not be rejected. This further confirms that the test results remain statistically consistent across different runs.

3.2.5 Conclusion

Extractive summarization extracts important or relevant sentences in a document as the corresponding summary. In this work, we have presented a new method XSumm-PSO for extractive single document summarization in English language. We propose to represent each sentence by ten features and score a sentence against those features with a suitable weight. These feature weights show the importance of each feature and also help to generate the summaries. The resultant summaries generated by the proposed method covered a significant portion of the relevant contents without "Incorrect word " when compared with the human-authored summaries. Here, we extracted 30% sentences from the document in the form of resultant summaries. Statistical test is also conducted to ensure that the results are consistent across various runs.

3.3 Enhancing Extractive Summarization using Supervised DPSO approach with Fluency Score and Feature Enhancements

The contributions of this work are as follows:

(1) We present XSumm-DPSO, a supervised dynamic PSO technique for fine-tuning individual feature weights. By utilizing gold standard summaries, this supervised approach improves the effectiveness of feature weight optimization.

These optimized weights are subsequently used to rank the sentences based on their importance within the document. Notably, this innovative approach marks the first application of a DPSO-based method in a supervised setting for extractive text summarization, establishing a pioneering milestone in the field. (2) We introduce a feature called "Fluency Score" to identify sentences in the document that contain grammaratically correct. (3) The experimental results show that the proposed XSumm-DPSO approach, incorporating the "Fluency Score feature, delivers notable performance gains over state-of-the-art extractive summarization methods. On the DUC 2002 dataset, it achieves improvements of +3.05% in ROUGE-1 and +1.76% in ROUGE-2 scores. Similarly, on the CNN/DailyMail dataset, the approach yields even greater enhancements +4.41% for ROUGE-1, +6.99% for ROUGE-2, and +3.76% for ROUGE-L demonstrating its effectiveness and robustness across different benchmark datasets. (4) Validation through a t-test confirmed that the proposed approach delivers statistically consistent results across multiple runs.

The remainder of this approach is organized as follows: Sub-section 3.3.1 elaborates on the proposed methodology; Sub-section 3.3.2 presents the experimental and controlling parameters; Sub-section 3.3.3 discusses the results; Sub-section 3.3.4 presents the one-sample t-test; and Sub-section 3.3.5 provides the conclusion.

3.3.1 Proposed methodology

3.3.1.1 Problem statement

The aim of the extractive text summarization assignment is to produce a summary by selecting and extracting the L most critical sentences from the source text, according to their ranking and importance. In this case, the document's length N is always more than the summary's L length. Let each document D be represented as a sequence of sentences, $s_j = (s_1, s_2, s_3, ...s_N)$, where $1 <= j <= N$. Each jth sentence is represented by a 19-dimensional feature vector $f_j = (f_{j1}, f_{j2}, f_{j3}, ..., f_{j19})$. The proposed XSumm-DPSO optimization algorithm assigns a weight to each of the 19 feature values. Feature weights are represented as $w_j = (w_{j1}, w_{2j}, w_{j3}, ..., w_{j19})$. This weight captures the relative importance of the corresponding feature towards the overall score of a sentence. The overall score of a sentence is the sum of products of its feature values and the corresponding feature weights, i.e., $s_j = w_{j1} * f_{j1} + w_{j2} * f_{j2} +, ..., +w_{j19} * f_{j19}$. The top-$L$ scoring sentences eventually form the summary of the document.

The proposed method, illustrated in Figure 3.4, comprises five main stages: (i) preprocessing, (ii) feature extraction, (iii) feature weight estimation using the XSumm-DPSO algorithm, (iv) sentence scoring and ranking, and (v) extractive summary generation. Each of these stages is described in detail below.

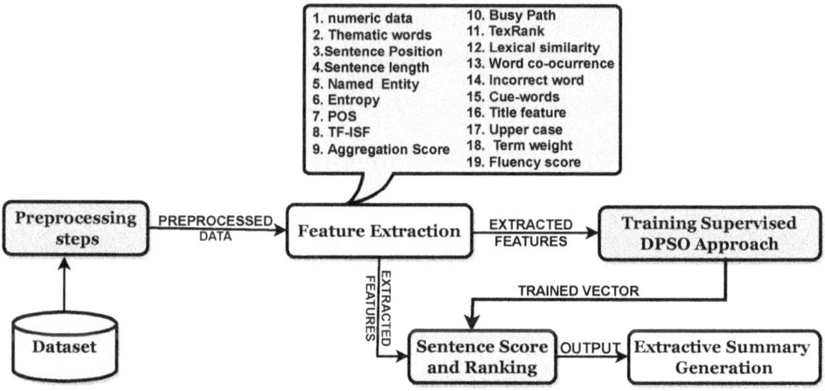

FIGURE 3.4: Text-based extractive summarization using non-static PSO

3.3.1.2 Pre-processing stage

Preprocessing allows for the transformation of the raw data or text into a more appropriate format for further analysis or modelling. We have tokenized the sentences of our documents using NLTK[8] sentence tokenizer. The tokenised sentences are further tokenized into tokens using a space delimiter. The stop words[9] and punctuation of English are removed from those tokens. The tokens are further converted to their root form using popular stemmer/lemmatization[10] (WordNetLemmatizer).

3.3.1.3 Feature Extraction

During feature extraction, 19 features are extracted from each sentence of a preprocessed document. These features are described next. The subscript Dj in each

[8]https://www.nltk.org/api/nltk.tokenize.html
[9]https://www.geeksforgeeks.org/removing-stop-words-nltk-python/
[10]https://www.geeksforgeeks.org/python-lemmatization-with-nltk/

feature indicates that the feature is being computed for the jth sentence of the Dth document.

1. **Numeric Data (ND_{Dj}):** Numerical values appearing in a sentence often serve as significant indicator of important information such as dates, monetary amounts, or quantities, which ultimately elevate the importance of the sentence for inclusion in the document summary. In this context, the Numerical data feature quantifies the presence of numeric values within a sentence by normalizing the count of numeric values against the highest count found among all the sentences in a document.

2. **Thematic Words (TW_{Dj}):** Thematic words are words that appear frequently in a document and express the main idea. These words help in determining the importance of the sentence. If the number of thematic words in a sentence increases, the importance of the sentence will increase. First the words are ranked on the basis of their frequency of appearance. Then, the top 50% most frequent words are considered as the set of thematic words. Let the total number of thematic words in the jth sentence be denoted by twc_{Dj}. Let the highest number of thematic terms in any sentence in the Dth document be denoted by $twcMax_D$. The thematic terms feature is scored as per Equation 3.16.

$$TW_{Dj} = \frac{twc_{Dj}}{twcMax_D} \tag{3.16}$$

3. **Sentence Position (SP_{Dj}):** It has been observed that sentences near the beginning and ending of a document tend to contain more significant facts than sentences in the middle of the document. The sentence position feature emphasises the importance of a sentence's location with respect to its proximity to the document's two ends. It is calculated using Equation 3.17.

$$SP_{Dj} = \frac{|\frac{N_D}{2} - j|}{\frac{N_D}{2}} \tag{3.17}$$

where, N_D refers the total sentences in the Dth document.

4. **Sentence Length (SL_{Dj}):** Very small sentences convey less information and context, reducing their informational value. On the other hand, very long sentences may contain a lot of excessive or unnecessary information.

Thus, it is advisable to choose sentences that are of average length. The sentence length feature calculates the proximity of a sentence's length to the average sentence length within a specific document. It is calculated as per Equation 3.18:

$$SL_{jD} = 1 - \frac{|AvgL_D - L_{Dj}|}{maxL_D} \tag{3.18}$$

where,
$AvgL_D$ is the average of the maximum and minimum length of any sentence in the Dth document,
L_{Dj} is the length of the jth sentence in the Dth document, and
$maxL_D$ is the maximum length of any sentence in the Dth document.

5. **Name Entity (NE_{Dj}):** The named entity feature aims to highlight the importance of named entities, such as places, people, things, groups of people, and times in summarizing a document. These entities play an important role in any document and are likely to be included in its summary. The feature value for each sentence in the document is computed as given in Equation 3.19:

$$NE_{Dj} = \frac{nec_{Dj}}{necMax_D} \tag{3.19}$$

where,
nec_{Dj} is the number of named entities in the jth sentence of the Dth document and
$necMax_D$ represents the highest number of named entities present in any single sentence within the Dth document.

6. **Part of Speech (NV_{Dj}):** The purpose of the part of speech feature is to highlight the important roles of nouns and verbs, which are essential sentence building blocks and significantly affect whether or not a sentence will be included in the document summary. This feature focuses on whether nouns and verbs are present in a sentence in the document. Each sentence's feature value is calculated as given by Equation 3.20:

$$NV_{Dj} = \frac{nvc_{Dj}}{nvcMax_D} \tag{3.20}$$

where,
nvc_{DJ} denotes the total count of nouns and verbs in the jth sentence of the Dth document and

$nvcMax_D$ represents the maximum combined count of nouns and verbs in any single sentence within the Dth document.

7. **Entropy (EN_{Dj}):** The entropy-based feature is designed to quantify the element of surprise or uncertainty associated with the occurrence of a word in a document. The main idea is that rare words are more surprising because they have low probabilities of occurring, while common words are less surprising because they have high probabilities. Entropy feature for each sentence in the document is computed using Equation 3.21.

$$EN_{Dj} = \sum_{w \in W_{jD}} -(p(w) * log_2(p(w))) \tag{3.21}$$

where, W_{jD} denotes the set of words in the jth sentence of the Dth document.

8. **TF-ISF ($TF\text{-}ISF_{Dj}$):** The TF-ISF (term frequency-inverse sentence frequency) feature builds upon the well-known TF-IDF (term frequency-inverse document frequency) score of a word. While the IDF is calculated at the document level, the ISF is calculated at the sentence level. The ISF of a term t in the jth sentence of the Dth document, denoted $ISF_{Dj}(t)$, is computed as per Equation 3.22:

$$ISF_{Dj}(t) = log(\frac{N_D}{sn_D(t)}) \tag{3.22}$$

where,
N_D is the total number of sentences in the Dth document, and
$sn_D(t)$ is the number of sentences in the Dth document containing the term t.

Then, the TF-ISF for the term t in the jth sentence of the Dth document, denoted $TF\text{-}ISF_{Dj}(t)$, is computed as per Equation 3.23:

$$TF\text{-}ISF_{Dj}(t) = TF_D(t) * ISF_{Dj}(t) \tag{3.23}$$

where, $TF_D(t)$ denotes the term-frequency of the term t in the Dth document.

Further, the TF-ISF of the jth sentence of the ith document, denoted $TF\text{-}ISF_{Dj}$, is computed as the sum of TF-ISF values of its constituent words. $TF\text{-}ISF_{Dj}$ is the final output that is used as a feature.

9. **Aggregation Score (AS_{Dj}):** This feature measures how similar a sentence is to the other sentences in the document. Let V_D be the vocabulary for the Dth document. The jth sentence in the Dth document is then represented as a vector of size $|V_D|$, where the ith element in the vector is the TF-ISF value of the corresponding word in the jth sentence calculated as per Equation 3.23. Then, the aggregate score (AS_{Dj}) feature value for the jth sentence in the Dth document is defined as the sum of the similarity scores of the sentence with other sentences in the document, where the similarity between two sentences is calculated by computing the cosine similarity between their respective vector representations.

10. **Busy Path (BP_{Dj}):** This feature is calculated using cosine similarity scores between two sentences and their corresponding vectors, such as TF-IDF, as mentioned in the above two features. The similarity scores are converted to binary values using a threshold of 0.7. If a similarity score is greater than 0.7, it is assigned a value of 1; otherwise, it is assigned a value of 0. Then, the count of zero similarity scores for each sentence is normalized by dividing them by the maximum zero count of any sentence in the document.

11. **TextRank (TR_{Dj}):** The textRank is a graph-based ranking method derived by utilizing pagerank that is used to extract significant keywords and estimate their weight over the entire document using a graph model. Sentences with a large number of pertinent keywords receive a better score using this strategy. The score of a word, which is a vertex in the graph, is evaluated as presented in Equation 3.24.

$$TR_{v_i} = (1-d) + d * \sum_{v_c \in In(v_i)} \frac{w_{ci}}{\sum_{v_k \in Out(v_c)} w_{ck}} * TR_{v_c} \tag{3.24}$$

where,
d is the damping factor, typically set to 0.85,
$In(v_i)$ is the set of nodes with outgoing edges to v_c,
$Out(v_c)$ is the set of nodes with incoming edges from v_c, and
w_{ci} is the total of co-occurrences in v_i and v_c.
$TextRank_{v_c}$ returns the textRank weight of a term or n-gram v_c.
Then, the textrank score of a sentence is the sum of scores of its constituent words as per Equation 3.24.

12. **Lexical Similarity (LS_{Dj}):** Lexical similarity is predicated on the idea that significant sentences are composed of powerful word chains, e.g., words that have a certain kind of relation, such as synonymy. By giving sentences with strong chains more weight, this approach determines how similar the words in a sentence are to one another. Typically, the WordNet[11] is utilised to determine the semantic relationships between words. The lexical similarity for a sentence in a document is computed as the ratio of the number of strong chains in the sentences to the maximum number of strong chains in any sentence in the document.

13. **Word Co-occurrence (WC_{Dj}):** A sequence of n words is called an n-gram. This feature captures the co-occurrence of n-grams in a sentence with respect to other sentences in the documents. First, the co-occurrence score between the jth sentence in the Dth document is computed as per Equation 3.25:

$$WC_{Dj} = \sum_{j=1, i \neq j}^{N_D} CountNgram(S_i, S_j) \tag{3.25}$$

where,
$CountNgram(S_i, S_j)$ is number of common n-grams between S_i (i^{th} sentence in the document) and S_j (j^{th} sentence in the document), and
N_D is the number of sentences in the Dth document.

The WC_{Dj} value is then normalized by dividing it by the maximum possible co-occurrence score of any sentence in the document.

14. **Cue Words (CW_{Dj}):** In this feature, for each sentence, we evaluate each word to determine if it meets specific criteria to be considered a cue word. The criteria include: Words starting with “in" or “the", and Words in the provided list (e.g., “firstly", “secondly", “thirdly", “lastly", “finally", “also", “furthermore", “indeed", “certainly", “especially", “in fact", “notably", “particularly", “in conclusion", “to sum up", “overall", “therefore", “in summary", “all in all", “for instance", “for example", “such as", “like", “in particular", “particular", “specifically", “first", “second", “then", “next", “after", “before", “meanwhile", “finally", “eventually", “now", “because", “since", “as a result", “result", “consequently", “therefore", “thus", “hence", “so", “due to", “like", “similarly", “likewise", “in the same way", “as", “compared to",

[11] https://www.geeksforgeeks.org/nlp-synsets-for-a-word-in-wordnet/

"on the contrary", "best", "most", "important", "and", "also", "furthermore", "moreover", "in addition", "besides", "as well", "similarly", "but", "however", "nevertheless", "yet", "on the other hand", "whereas", "although", "despite", "instead" etc.). We then count the cue words for each sentence in the document and normalize each count by dividing it by the maximum count.

15. **Upper Case** (UC_{Dj})**:** In this features, count the term for each sentence in the document D, if term is entirely upper case. Then divided the count of upper case of each sentence by highest count of upper case of any sentence in the document.

16. **Title Match** (TF_{Dj}) **:** In this feature, we utilize the LDA model to identify a single topic represented by a set of ten words, which serves as the document title. We then score each sentence in the document based on the frequency of title words it contains. Finally, we normalize the scores by dividing them by the maximum score of any sentence in the document.

17. **Term-Weight** (TW_{Dj})**:** In this features, we count the each term in the document D, and divided each term by highest count of term. Sentences are score by adding the term weight having those terms belongs in the sentences.

18. **Incorrect Word** (IW_{Dj})**:** The typographical or spelling mistakes in a sentence are termed as "Incorrect word". Even though improper terms might be present in the original text, it's extremely improbable that they would be chosen for the gold-standard human-authored summary. Therefore, the likelihood that a sentence will be chosen in the equivalent gold-standard human-authored extracted summary of the document decreases when the sentence has incorrect words. This inspired us to develop a feature called "Incorrect word" that detects the presence of misspelled words. The "Incorrect word" feature value for a sentence is calculated by dividing the number of misspelled words (with negatives values) in the sentence by the highest number of misspelled words in any sentence within the document. To our knowledge, this is the first instance of using a feature of this nature to evaluate a sentence's relevance for inclusion in a document's extracted summary.

19. **Fluency Score** (FS_{Dj})**:** In this feature, we compute the fluency score for each sentence in a document based on GPT-2-based perplexity. A pre-trained GPT-2 language model is employed to calculate the loss for a given sentence, which is then transformed into perplexity using the exponential

function exp(loss). The fluency score serves as a measure of how natural, grammatically correct, and coherent a sentence is. It reflects the likelihood that a language model (such as GPT-2) would generate or accept the sentence as valid human language. This score is derived from perplexity, as shown in Equation 3.26:

$$\text{Fluency Score} = \frac{1}{\text{Perplexity}} \tag{3.26}$$

A higher fluency score (closer to 1) indicates greater fluency, while nonsensical or ungrammatical sentences yield lower scores. By inverting the perplexity, we obtain a bounded and interpretable metric that can effectively identify incoherent or unnatural language in machine-generated text.

The above features are extracted for every sentence in a document. These are weighted by some weights which are determined through a DPSO algorithm. Using these relative weights, the above features are used again to score the sentences in a document in order to generate the extractive summaries.

3.3.1.4 XSumm-DPSO

The XSumm-DPSO framework approach is shown in Fig. 3.5 and the features are optimized based on given Algorithm 1. The XSumm-DPSO methodology comprises of various components that collaborate to systematically explore the solution space for optimal results. The key components of XSumm-DPSO encompass the following stages: (1) Initialization, (2) Evaluation of the fitness function, (3) Identification of the current best solution, (4) Updating the velocity and position of each particle, and (5) Determining the termination criteria for the algorithm. Each of these components is elaborated upon in the following descriptions.

1. **Initialization**:- Initialization is the first step of XSumm-DPSO. We need to initialize parameters for this approach in the extractive text summarization. Here, we consider that each article behaves like a particle represented by Fig. 3.7. Each particle is associated with position vector (w) and velocity vector (v), both having dimensions equal to the number of features, which is also shown in Fig. 3.6, where the ith feature's position is w_i and i^{th} feature's velocity is v_i, i.e., $i \in \{1, 2, 3 \ldots 19\}$.

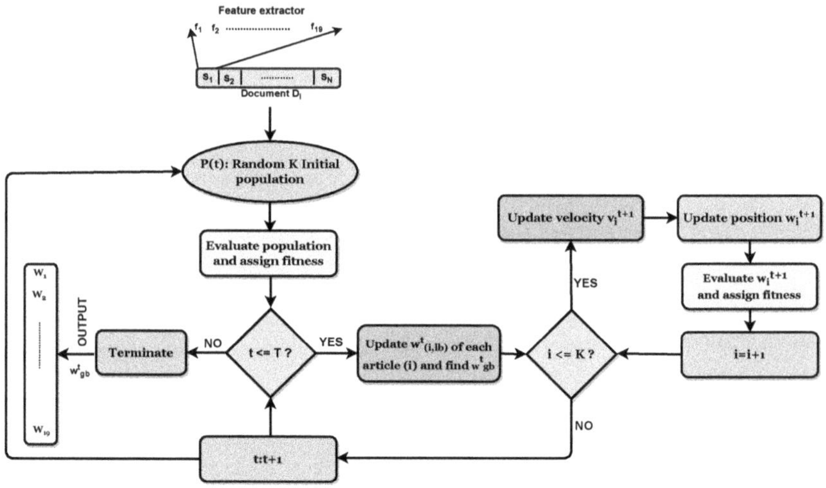

FIGURE 3.5: Text-based extractive summarization using non-static PSO

2. **Fitness function**:- In this stage, the document involves nineteen features of individual sentences, mirroring the format presented in Fig. 3.7. Every document has a positional vector associated with it (like the one in Fig. 3.6). The position vector is linearly transformed by multiplying it with the corresponding sentence features within a document. Sentences are selected from each document based on their weighted scores, which determine their relevance. The highest scoring L sentences are selected for evaluation based on the objective function given in Equation 3.27. BERTScore_recall serves as the fitness function for obtaining a precise quantitative measure. In this manner, we acquire K values for the objective function, with each solution having its own corresponding value. The solution deemed the best globally is identified as the one with the best fitness value.

$$R = \frac{1}{n} \sum_{j=1}^{n} \max_{i \in [1,m]} \text{sim}(r_j, c_i) \tag{3.27}$$

Where,

- R: Recall equation of BERTScore
- r_j: j^{th} token from the reference
- c_i: i^{th} token from the condidate
- sim(r_j, c_i): cosine similarity between BERT embeddings of tokens

3. **Finding the current best solution**:- Initially, the personal best positions $w^t(i, lb)$ and global best position $w^t(i, gb)$ are updated based on the current personal best position, which is identified as the one with the highest fitness value.

   (a) **Update local best position $w^t(i, lb)$ of each solution**: The local best position of the ith solution in the tth generation is denoted by $w^t(i, lb)$. We update this local best position, $w^t_{(i,lb)}$, using Equation (3.28) to optimize the objective function.

$$w^{t+1}_{(i,lb)} = \begin{cases} w_i^{t+1}, & \text{if } f(w_i^{t+1}) < f(w_i^t) \\ w_i^t, & otherwise \end{cases} \tag{3.28}$$

   (b) **Update global best position $w^t_{(i,gb)}$ of each solution:** To identify the globally optimal solution, it is essential to initially determine the individual optimal positions for each solution in the search space. Then, the solution with the personal best value that corresponds to the highest fitness value is designated as the global best position, denoted by $w^t(i, gb)$, for the tth generation. The global best position, $w^t_{(i,gb)}$, is then calculated using Equation 3.29.

$$w^t_{(i,gb)} \in \{w_i^t, ..., w_K^t\} | f(w^t_{(gb)}) = max\{f(w_i^t), ..., f(w_K^t)\} \tag{3.29}$$

   Here, K represents the number of particles within the population.

4. **Update velocity and position of each particle:** Initially, the velocity of a particle undergoes an update, followed by an adjustment of its position in accordance with the newly updated velocity.

   (a) **Update velocity v_i^t of each particle:-** The velocity of each feature value for every particle solution is updated by considering its current velocity according to the following procedure as given in Equation 3.30:

$$v_i^{t+1} = Wv_i^t + c_1 r_1 (w^t_{(i,lb)} - w_i^t) + c_2 r_2 (w^t_{(i,gb)} - w_i^t) \tag{3.30}$$

   where,

   - Wv_i^t: This part of the velocity is the momentum part. It makes the particle move in the same direction and with the same velocity. The parameter W is a inertia weight and here, it is a positive

dynamic changable for each iteration. It is crucial for maintaining equilibrium between the global search, known as exploitation (when lower values are set), and the global search, also known as exploration (when higher values are set).
$W = W_{max} - (W_{max} - W_{min}) * (\frac{i}{iteration})$

- Cognitive part $c_1 r_1 (w^t_{(i,lb)}\text{-}w^t_i)$: It represents personal influence to improve the particle. It also makes the particle return to a previous position, better than the current.
- Social part $c_2 r_2 (w^t_{(i,gb)}\text{-}w^t_i)$: It represents social influence and makes the particle follow the best neighbours direction.
- $w^t_{(i,lb)}$: The position that has been identified as the personal best so far.
- $w^t_{(i,gb)}$: The optimal position discovered globally within the neighbourhood of the document.
- v_i represents the velocity of the ith document.
- r_1 and r_2 denote two randomly selected numbers from a uniform distribution within the range [0, 1]. The coefficients of societal and personal acceleration are denoted by C_1 and C_2, respectively.

(b) **Update position p^t_i of each particle:-** The document's location, as denoted by its associated weight vector, is adjusted by considering its present velocity and its prior position as given in Equation 3.31.

$$w^{t+1}_i = w^t_i + v^{t+1}_i \tag{3.31}$$

In this context, p_i represents the current position of the document indexed as i within the population.

5. **Determining the termination**:- Every cycle involves repeating the previous stages. The total number of iterations is specified by the user. The optimization algorithm concludes its execution upon reaching this specified number of iterations. Following this, the global best position vector is generated, and it is subsequently utilized for testing purposes. It is represented as $w_D = w^1_D, w^2_D, w^3_D.....w^{19}_D$.

3.3.1.5 Sentence Scoring and Ranking

Each sentence in every document is assigned a score calculated by the formula: $w_{Dj} = w^1Dj * f^1Dj + ... + w^{19}Dj * f^{19}Dj$. The sentences are then ranked according to their calculated scores.

3.3.1.6 Extractive Summary Generation

Following the sentence ranking process, resultant summaries are generated by choosing the top C= 30% sentences of the articles.

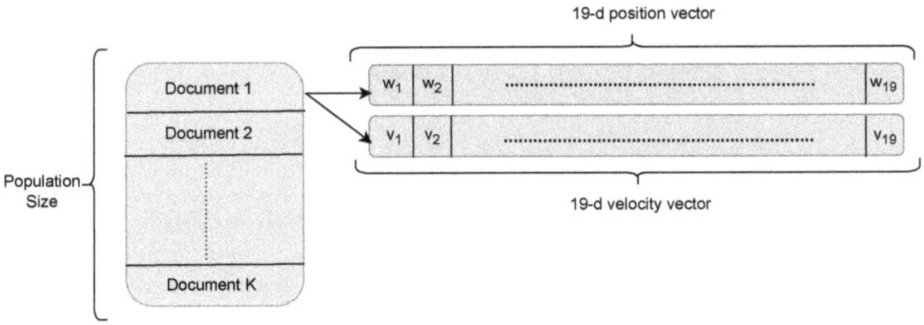

FIGURE 3.6: Diagram of position and velocity representation

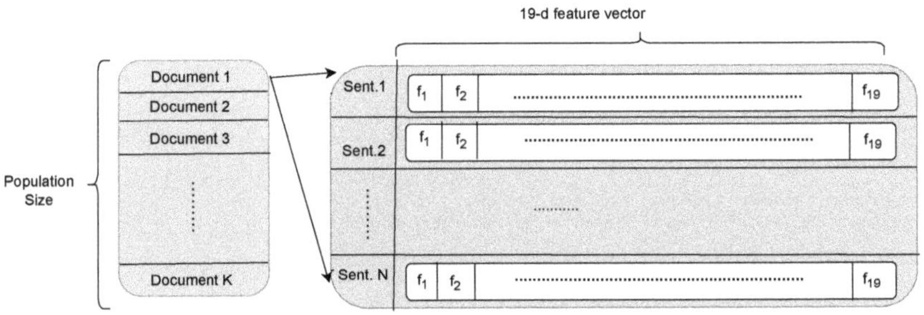

FIGURE 3.7: Diagram of particle representation

3.3.2 Experimental Setup

This section evaluates our suggested methodology using two benchmark datasets (as described in Section 2.2.1 and presented in Table 2.1) with varying controlling

Algorithm 1: Assign features weight optimization (XSumm-DPSO) algorithm

Input: Inilaization: w_i and v_i are position and velocity of ith feature, maximum iteration for selection sample (T), $w_{(i,lb)}$, $w_{(i,gb)}$, generate random particles (K) and objective function ($BERT\_recall$), iterations=10, $W_{max} = 0.9$, $W_{min} = 0.4$

Output: $w_i = w_i^1, w_i^2, w_i^3.....w_i^{19}$;

for *batch := 1 to T* **do**
  while $i <$ *iteration* **do**
    $W = W_{max} - (W_{max} - W_{min}) * (i/iteration)$
    for *i := 1 to K* **do**
      $f_{w_i} = f(w_i)$ using Equation 3.27
      if $f_{w_i} > f(w_{(i,lb)})$ **then**
        $w_i(i, lb) = w_i$;
      $w(i, gb)$= best w_i in K;
    for *i := 1 to K* **do**
      $v_i^{t+1} = W_x.v_i^t + c_1.r_1(w_{(i,lb)}\text{-}w_i) + c_2.r_2(w_{(i,gb)}\text{-}w_i)$;
      $w_i^{t+1} = w_i^t + v_i^{t+1}$
  i = i+1
return $w(i, gb) = w_i^1, w_i^2, w_i^3.....w_i^{19}$;

parameter configurations (described in Section 3.3.2.1). Furthermore, we juxtaposed the acquired outcomes with those of modern, cutting-edge methodologies. Additionally, we used statistical techniques to look at the results' consistency.

3.3.2.1 Controlling parameters

Here, the proposed methodology is applied to conduct extractive single-document summarization on two benchmark datasets: CNN/DailyMail and DUC-2002, for training purpose, various controlling parameters are given in Table 3.10. The optimal values often depend on the specific problem being solved. Parameter fine tuning is typically done through experimentation and may involve running the algorithm with different combinations to find the set that works best for a particular optimization problem.

3.3.3 Results

In this section, the experimental results on the proposed framework is compared with the contemporary state-of-the-art methods using ROUGE (metrics discussed

TABLE 3.10: Controlling parameters setting.

Parameters	**Value**
Iteration (T)	1000
Dimension size (d)	19
Population size (K)	20
W_{max}	.9
W_{min}	.4
c1	1
c2	1
Random number	(0,1)

under the section 2.1) scores, as shown in Tables 3.13 and 3.14. XSumm-DPSO demonstrated high accuracy in the context of single-document extractive summarization on the CNN/DailyMail and DUC-2002 datasets. Our approach is an iterative and randomized approach because of which we have reported results averaged over ten random runs for CNN/DailyDaily and DUC-2002 datasets in Tables 3.13 and 3.14, respectively. XSumm-DPSO surpassed all the evaluated state-of-the-art methods with its ROUGE-1, ROUGE-2, and ROUGE-L scores of 49.79%, 28.10% and 44.80%, respectively, for CNN/DailyMail dataset. The same set of results on the DUC-2002 dataset are 65.32%, 34.75%, and 40.16% respectively.

It must be noted that none of the state-of-the art summarization approaches have used all the 18 features (i.e., excluding the newly proposed "Fluency Score" feature from the set of 19) for document summarization - either on DUC-2002 dataset (Sup-NN-T [62], ESDS_SMODE [51], ESDS-ABCDE [44], DeepSumm [48], WL-Attention_FT [74], PSOGA-BKSum [52], ETS-MBCSO [50]) or on CNN/DailyMail dataset (Sub+Lex+LSA+RR [87], WL-AttenSumm_W2V [74], DeepSumm [48]). Further, neither of these summarizers capture grammatically correct sentences and generate summaries with Fluency Score. However, our model captures grammaticaly correct sentences using "Fluency Score" feature. Due to all this, our proposed framework produces superior results than existing works.

Table 3.11 illustrates a sample summary produced by the proposed method for a document from DUC-2002 dataset. Table 3.12 displays a representative summary generated by the XSumm-DPSO method for a CNN/DailyMail document. The objective of our research was two fold: to evaluate the effectiveness of our introduced "Fluency Score" feature and to evaluate the effectiveness of the proposed DPSO. We started our experiment without the Fluency Score feature with DPSO and found that the ROUGE scores for 1 gram, 2 gram and L (longest common subsequence) were 46.59%, 25.01% and 42.75% , respectively, on CNN/DailyMail dataset. The experiment was repeated by excluding the "Fluency Score" feature resulting in ROUGE-1, ROUGE-2 and ROUGE-L scores of 64.8%, 33.2% and 39.3%, respectively, on DUC-2002 dataset. The results are shown in Tables 3.13 and 3.14. In our second experiment, we evaluated the performance of the DPSO optimization approach for weight estimation in a supervised manner with "Fluency Score" feature, we achieved ROUGE-1, ROUGE-2 and ROUGE-L scores of 49.79 %, 28.10%, and 44.80%, respectively for CNN/DailyMail dataset. We repeated this experiment for DUC-2002 and found the ROUGE-1, ROUGE-2, and ROUGE-L scores of 65.32%, 34.75% and 40.16%. These results are shown in Tables 3.13 and 3.14 in bold letters highlighted the results of PSO.

3.3.3.1 Discussion

The major finding of the current research is that the inclusion of fluency score as features with XSumm-DPSO improves the quality of system generated summaries as evident by the improved ROUGE scores and manual inspection. The reason being that the fluency score feature scoring the sentences having them, increase their chances of being included the generated summary. Unlike previous static PSO framework [7], which relies on fixed control parameters throughout the optimization process, Dynamic PSO (DPSO) adaptively adjusts key parameters such as inertia weight during the search. This dynamic adjustment allows DPSO to better align with different search phases, promoting stronger global exploration in early iterations and more effective local exploitation in later stages. As a result, DPSO typically achieves faster convergence compared to static PSO. Furthermore, by maintaining adaptive parameter control, DPSO reduces the risk of premature convergence and stagnation in local optima by preserving population diversity. This adaptive behavior enables DPSO to identify higher-quality and more robust optimal solutions and enhances its robustness across diverse optimization landscapes and problem complexities.

This improves the quality of the generated summary. The current research outperformed the state-of-the-art models in single document extractive summarization. The state-of-the-art result is obtained by Singh et al. [7] on CNN/DailyMail dataset achieving ROUGE-1, 2 and L scores of 45.30 %, 21.11% and 41.04%, respectively. Our model outperformed that even without using the "Fluency Score"

TABLE 3.11: Gold summary and XSumm-DPSO generated for a document from DUC 2002 dataset.

XSumm-DPSO
Ousted East German leader Erich Honecker will not stand trial in East Germany as long as the formerly Communist country exists, a West German newspaper reported. However, Seidel said that the investigation was not far enough along to determine whether charges could be filed against Honecker before East Germany merges with West Germany on Oct. He is under investigation on allegations of abuse of power, corruption, harboring terrorists and issuing shoot-to-kill orders to prevent East Germans from escaping to West Germany when he served as the country's leader. Negotiators are still working out the merger of the two German legal systems.
Gold summary
A West German newspaper reported that ousted East German leader Erich Honecker will not stand trial in East Germany as long as the formerly Communist country exists, although he could be prosecuted in a united Germany for violation of property laws. Honecker allegedly used $ 42 million for stocking a private housing estate for Communist government leaders. However, the investigation is not far enough along to determine whether charges would be filed against Honecker before the East German-West German merger. He is under investigation for abuse of power, corruption, harboring terrorists, and issuing shoot-to-kill orders against East Germans escaping to West Germany.

feature, producing improvements of +1.21%, +3.9% and +1.71% with respect to ROUGE-1, 2 and L scores, respectively. One the same metrics, our model outperforms with "Fluency Score" feature, producing improvements of +4.41%, +6.99% and +3.76% for ROUGE-1, ROUGE-2 and ROUGE-L, respectively. Another state-of-the-art result was obtained by Debnath et al. [50] on DUC 2002 dataset achieving ROUGE-1, 2 scores of 62.27%, 32.2%, respectively. Our proposed model outperformed without the use of "Fluency Score" feature, producing improvements of +2.53%, +.21% in terms of ROUGE-1, ROUGE-2, respectively. For DUC-2002 dataset, our model outperforms with "Fluency Score" feature, producing improvements of +3.05%, +1.76% for ROUGE-1, ROUGE-2.

3.3.4 Statistical significance t-test

To establish the statistical consistency of the results achieved through the proposed model XSumm-DPSO, we performed t-test [51] [50] at a significance level of 5%. The t-test yields t-statistical values, and a lower t-statistical value indicates greater statistical significance of our result. In this t-test, two hypothesis are taken into consideration: null hypothesis and an alternative hypothesis. The

TABLE 3.12: Gold summary and XSumm-DPSO generated for a document from CNN/DailyMail dataset.

XSumm-DPSO
Caught on camera: Leia, an eight-month-old Boxer from Pennsylvania, was filmed as she lay on the couch and latched on to a baby's pacifier. This has made my night, one fan exclaimed, while another added: 'That is the cutest thing I've ever seen! 'Nodding off: Footage shows her then sucking on it before closing her eyes and loudly snoring in her sleep. To date the video of Leia has garnered more than 145,000 likes on Facebook, with many viewers deeming the scene 'cute' and 'adorable'.
Gold summary
Leia, an eight-month-old Boxer from Pennsylvania, was filmed as she lay on the couch and latched on to a baby's pacifier. Footage shows her then sucking on it before closing her eyes and loudly snoring in her sleep. To date the video of Leia has garnered more than 145,000 likes on Facebook, with many viewers deeming the scene 'cute' and 'adorable'.

TABLE 3.13: Comparative study using CNN/DailyMail dataset between the suggested XSumm-DPSO model and other cutting-edge methods.

Method	ROUGE-1	ROUGE-2	ROUGE-L
Sub+Lex+LSA+RR [87]	23.06	09.29	21.08
WL-AttenSumm_W2V [74]	32.80	11.00	27.50
DeepSumm [48]	43.30	19.00	38.90
XSumm-PSO [7]	45.38	21.11	41.04
XSumm-DPSO(-)"Fluency Score"	46.59	25.01	42.75
XSumm-DPSO	**49.79**	**28.10**	**44.80**

TABLE 3.14: Analysis of the suggested XSumm-DPSO model in comparison to other cutting-edge methods using the DUC-2002 dataset.

Method	ROUGE-1	ROUGE-2	ROUGE-L
Sup-NN-T [62]	44.48	19.52	-
ESDS_SMODE [51]	49.12	34.13	-
ESDS-ABCDE [44]	52.33	30.23	-
DeepSumm [48]	53.20	28.70	49.20
WL-AttenSumm_FT [74]	55.90	24.80	53.90
XSumm-PSO [7]	55.9	29.5	50.0
PSOGA-BKSum [52]	56.99	27.50	52.34
ETS-MBCSO [50]	62.27	32.99	-
XSumm-DPSO(-)"Fluency Score"	64.8	33.2	39.3
XSumm-DPSO	**65.32**	**34.75**	**40.16**

null hypothesis posits that there is no notable difference between the test results accross various runs. On the other hand, the alternative hypothesis suggests a significant difference in the test results. One tail or t-test is considered here to calculate t-statistical value for three groups named as ROUGE-1, ROUGE-2 and ROUGE-L which contain list of scores produced by our approach across various runs. The t-statistical values for both datasets obtained are: (a) using ROUGE-1, ROUGE-2 and ROUGE-L for DUC-2002 are 0.120, 0.014, and 0.210. (b) using ROUGE-1, ROUGE-2 and ROUGE-L for CNN/DailyMail are 1.072, 0.272, and 2.243. The test results provide support for the hypothesis that the outcomes obtained from the proposed model did not occur by chance, test results does not very significantly accross various runs.

Upon comparing the t-statistic with the critical t-value (2.35) at a significance level alpha = 5%, we observed that the t-statistic to be lower than the critical t-value. As a result, the absence of sufficient evidence prevents us from rejecting the null hypothesis, indicating that there is no statistically significant difference between the sample mean and the population mean.

3.3.5 Conclusion

This work introduces an approach for single-document text summarization, namely XSumm-DPSO . Our proposal involves representing each sentence using nineteen distinct features and evaluating the sentences importance based on these features with appropriate weights. The weights assigned to these features indicate their significance and play a crucial role in generating the summaries using XSumm-DPSO approach. In this context, we have taken top 30% of the sentences from the document to form the resulting summaries. When compared to several cutting-edge methods, the results show how successful the recommended strategy is. Furthermore, readers find the summaries produced by the algorithm to be comprehensible and clear. To ensure reliability, a statistical test is also performed to verify the consistency of the outcomes across multiple iterations or runs.

Chapter 4

Single Document Extractive Summarization Using ML with Node2Vec techniques

The objectives of this chapter are following [1]:

- To introduce ML regression models for generating extractive summaries.
- To discuss the importance of Node2Vec feature extracted for each sentence in the article.
- To examine the proposed model using Indian language named: Hindi and Gujarati.

4.1 Introduction

In this study, we focus on the ILSUM-2022 task for Hindi and Gujarati languages. Our observations show in the literature that Transformer-based models are widely used for text summarization tasks. Among them: PEGASUS [102, 130], BART [130], T5 [130], and ProphetNet [130] have been fine-tuned for summarization, and PEGASUS performs best for English. For Hindi, a fine-tuned IndicBART [102, 103] model with augmented data has shown effective results. For Gujarati,

[1]The content of this chapter is based on [Accepted]

a fine-tuned PEGASUS [102] model combined with a translation mapping-based approach has been employed. Furthermore, K-means clustering with autoencoders and Word2Vec has been applied for extractive text summarization (ETS) in Hindi and English [28].

Multilingual Transformer-based models [104] such as mT5, MBart, and IndicBART are also used for abstractive summarization in Hindi, Gujarati, and English. A more detailed discussion of these methods is provided in Chapter 2.

We are motivated by building upon previous works for Hindi and Gujarati languages, we have identified two key gaps in existing research: (1) ML regression models have not been utilized for sentence ranking, and (2) Node2Vec [2] [131] features, obtained through random walk algorithms followed by Word2Vec [3] [132], have not been explored in feature extraction techniques for summarization tasks. Node2Vec generates embeddings that preserve the semantic relationships between nodes in a graph. It is useful for identifying key sentences or phrases that are central to the meaning of the document. It also enhanced feature representation; unlike traditional graph-based methods, Node2Vec generates dense, continuous feature representations that are more suitable for ML and DL models, improving downstream performance. Node2Vec is domain-agnostic and can be applied to any text type, from news articles to scientific papers. So, we propose a supervised framework called XSumm-ML, which integrates the Node2Vec features with machine learning regression models for extractive single-document text summarization. The key contributions of this work are:

- We employ supervised ML regression models to rank sentences within a document for extractive text summarization in Section 4.2.4. This method allows us to assess the importance of each sentence and create a concise summary in Section 4.2.5, effectively retaining the core information of the original document.
- We extracted semantic features from the article using Node2Vec, which combines a second-order random walk with Word2Vec. These Node2Vec features encapsulate the contextual relationships between words in the article and represent them as vector embeddings, as discussed in the section 4.2.2.

[2] https://keras.io/examples/graph/node2vec_movielens/
[3] https://www.tensorflow.org/text/tutorials/word2vec

- We evaluated the proposed model on Hindi and Gujarati, two Indian languages, as well as on English using the DUC-2002 dataset to assess its performance and robustness, as discussed in Section 4.4.

- As a result of the proposed supervised ML regression-based approach, XSumm-ML_RFR achieves ROUGE-1, ROUGE-2, and ROUGE-L scores of 60.0%, 42.0%, and 52.0%, respectively, outperforming state-of-the-art ETS methods on the Hindi dataset. Similarly, the Gujarati dataset, attains scores of 47.0%, 29.4%, and 41.0% for the same metrics, as detailed in Section 4.4.

4.1.1 Research Impact

The impact of our research extends beyond just the technical achievement of improved summarization scores. Our approach, XSumm-ML_RFR, not only sets a new benchmark in extractive summarization for low-resource languages, but also paves the way for more accessible and equitable technology solutions in linguistic diversity:

- **Inclusion of Underrepresented Languages**: By focusing on Hindi and Gujarati, languages typically underrepresented in NLP research, our work contributes to reducing the digital divide and promoting language inclusion in AI technologies.

- **Adaptability to Various Domains**: The robustness and effectiveness of our node2vec feature extraction and regression model approach demonstrate potential adaptability across different domains, from academic to legal texts, thus broadening the applicability of our research.

- **Foundation for Future Enhancements**: Our findings provide a solid foundation for future research, including the exploration of other low-resource languages and the integration of more complex NLP models, potentially enhancing both the accuracy and the efficiency of text summarization tools.

- **Practical Applications and Tool Development**: The improved summarization capabilities can lead to the development of practical tools for end-users, such as automated content summarizers in native apps, enhancing user engagement and content accessibility.

The remainder of this approach is organized as follows: Sub-section 4.2 elaborates on the proposed methodology; Sub-section 4.3 presents the experimental setup; Sub-section 4.4 discusses the results; and Sub-section 4.5 provides the conclusion.

4.2 Extractive summarization framework

This study proposes a multi-language summarization framework, called XSumm-ML_RFR, which combines node2vec features integrated into a machine learning regression model. The XSumm-ML_RFR framework consists of five phases, as illustrated in Fig. 4.1. The five phases are (i) pre-processing, (ii) feature extraction, (iii) creating labels, (iv) machine learning regression models, and (v) summary generation. Each phase is explained in detail in the following sections, providing a step-by-step overview of the XSumm-ML_RFR framework.

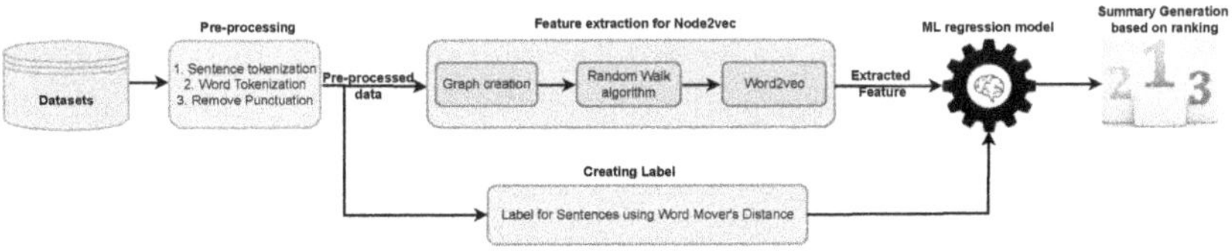

FIGURE 4.1: Architecture of Extractive Summarization Framework

4.2.1 Pre-processing

Pre-processing is an essential step in transforming raw text into a clean and structured format that is ready for further analysis. The following three steps are employed during pre-processing: (i) sentence tokenization, (ii) word tokenization, and (iii) punctuation removal. Sentence tokenization involves splitting the text into individual sentences using specific delimiters such as ["|", "."]. Word tokenization breaks text into words or tokens, typically using spaces as delimiters. This step is followed by the removal of unwanted empty strings and punctuation marks, such as [.,′, ?, !, ;, :, “, ”, ‘,′, (), [], −, ..., /, ;̂∗, &, _]. In addition, documents that contain three or fewer sentences are removed from the dataset.

4.2.2 Feature extraction

The feature extraction process begins by representing the article as a graph. A Node2Vec algorithm (using a second-order random walk) is applied to this graph, followed by the generation of contextual embeddings of each sentence using Word2Vec. This step consists of three modules, and each module is explained in detail below. For illustration, we take four sentences from Fig. 4.2 to demonstrate the approach.

```
This is computer system. Computer has software and hardware two parts.
How software interacts with hardware. How well software is developed
and designed.
```

FIGURE 4.2: This text demonstrates how the node2vec features can be represented in a numerical format.

1. **Graph creation:** Initially, we employed TF-IDF and cosine similarity, as shown in Equation 4.1, to represent the article in the graph. A graph is composed of a set of vertices (or nodes) and a set of edges (or links) that connect pairs of vertices. In this task, nodes represent sentences and the edge weights indicate similarities between the neighboring nodes, as illustrated in Fig. 4.3. TF-IDF is used to represent the sentences of the article in vector form, while cosine similarity is applied to calculate the similarity between sentences based on their TF-IDF vectors. These similarities ($\in (0, 1)$) are used to define the edges between two sentences, which helped remove weak or noisy connections while preserving meaningful semantic relationships. In this step, we also computed the sentence vectors and the cosine similarity matrix using the text provided in Fig. 4.2, as shown in Tables 4.1 4.2, respectively. This cosine similarity matrix is then converted into a graph, as illustrated in Fig. 4.3.

$$\text{cosine similarity} = \frac{S_1 \cdot S_2}{||\mathbf{S_1}||||\mathbf{S_2}||} \tag{4.1}$$

- $S_1 \cdot S_2$ is the dot product of context embedding of sentence S_1 and S_2 in same article.
- $||\mathbf{S_1}||$ and $||\mathbf{S_2}||$ are the magnitude of context embedding of Sentence S_1 and S_2.

TABLE 4.1: This is the TF-IDF vector representation of each sentence from the given text in Fig 4.2

Term	Sentence 1	Sentence 2	Sentence 3	Sentence 4
and	0.0	0.3434	0.0	0.3434
computer	0.4378	0.3434	0.0	0.0
designed	0.0	0.0	0.0	0.4355
developed	0.0	0.0	0.0	0.4355
hardware	0.0	0.3434	0.4126	0.0
has	0.0	0.4355	0.0	0.0
how	0.0	0.0	0.4126	0.3434
interacts	0.0	0.0	0.5234	0.0
is	0.4378	0.0	0.0	0.3434
parts	0.0	0.4355	0.0	0.0
software	0.0	0.2780	0.3341	0.2780
system	0.5553	0.0	0.0	0.0
this	0.5553	0.0	0.0	0.0
two	0.0	0.0	0.0	0.0
well	0.0	0.0	0.5234	0.0
with	0.0	0.0	0.0	0.0

TABLE 4.2: The cosine similarity matrix is derived using the vector representation of each sentence as shown in Table 4.1

	Sentence 1	Sentence 2	Sentence 3	Sentence 4
Sentence 1	1.0000	0.1503	0.0000	0.1503
Sentence 2	0.1503	1.0000	0.2346	0.1952
Sentence 3	0.0000	0.2346	1.0000	0.2346
Sentence 4	0.1503	0.1952	0.2346	1.0000

2. **Node2vec Features:** In the second step of feature extraction, we have applied a 2nd order random walk algorithm followed by the Word2Vec model on the created graph to extract the Node2Vec features. Finally, we have a graph with nodes and edges with weight. Further, we apply the 2nd order random walk [4][133] algorithm on this graph to extract the Node2Vec features for each sentence in the document. A 2nd Random Walk is a type of stochastic process where the next state depends on the two previous states, rather than just the last state (as in a first-order random walk). In a 2nd random walk in equation 4.2, the position at time t, denoted as R_t follows

[4]A second-order random walk is called so because it considers the previous step and the current step when deciding the next move in the walk. This adds a layer of dependency on the last transition, unlike a first-order random walk, the next step is chosen solely based on the current node, independent of the past.

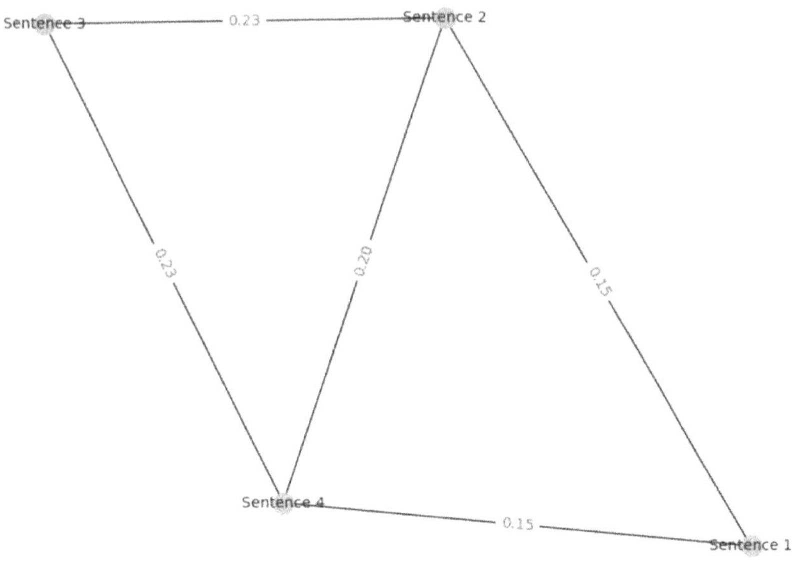

FIGURE 4.3: This graph is derived from Table 4.2 above, with a similarity range of (0,1)

the recurrence relation.

$$R_t = 2R_{t-1} - R_{t-2} + \epsilon_t \tag{4.2}$$

where,

- R_t is the state at time t.
- R_{t-1} and R_{t-2} are the two previous states.
- ϵ_t is a random noise term.

Random walk is a mathematical concept used to describe a path consisting of a series of random steps within a defined space, in which the direction or magnitude of each step is determined randomly. The random walk involves moving between nodes of a graph based on transition probabilities. In the proposed approach, we have used Continuous and 2D Random Walk. The walker moves continuously, with step sizes and directions drawn from a continuous distribution, because the similarity between the sentences is continuous, and steps taken on a plane (e.g. up, down, left, or right) are called 2D. Random walks on the graph learn node representations based on their “context" within walks. The result of a random walk algorithm is usually a sequence or list of nodes that were visited during the walk. It begins at the initial node and ends at the final node reached at the time of termination of the algorithm. The path generated by a random walk algorithm through the graph as shown in Fig. 4.4 looks like [“sentence 4", “sentence 3", “sentence 2", “sentence 1", “sentence 4"]. Here, we took, walks, and steps are 5 and 5 to show small demonstration in Fig. 4.4.

```
Random walks iteration 1 of 5: 100%|██████████| 4/4 [00:00<00:00, 1733.00it/s]
Random walks iteration 2 of 5: 100%|██████████| 4/4 [00:00<00:00, 2789.69it/s]
Random walks iteration 3 of 5: 100%|██████████| 4/4 [00:00<00:00, 2774.01it/s]
Random walks iteration 4 of 5: 100%|██████████| 4/4 [00:00<00:00, 2810.25it/s]
Random walks iteration 5 of 5: 100%|██████████| 4/4 [00:00<00:00, 2287.91it/s]
Generated Random Walks: 20
['Sentence 3', 'Sentence 4', 'Sentence 2', 'Sentence 1', 'Sentence 2']
['Sentence 4', 'Sentence 3', 'Sentence 2', 'Sentence 4', 'Sentence 1']
['Sentence 2', 'Sentence 4', 'Sentence 1', 'Sentence 2', 'Sentence 4']
['Sentence 1', 'Sentence 4', 'Sentence 1', 'Sentence 2', 'Sentence 3']
['Sentence 3', 'Sentence 2', 'Sentence 1', 'Sentence 4', 'Sentence 3']
['Sentence 2', 'Sentence 1', 'Sentence 4', 'Sentence 1', 'Sentence 2']
['Sentence 1', 'Sentence 4', 'Sentence 2', 'Sentence 4', 'Sentence 3']
['Sentence 4', 'Sentence 2', 'Sentence 3', 'Sentence 4', 'Sentence 2']
['Sentence 3', 'Sentence 2', 'Sentence 4', 'Sentence 3', 'Sentence 2']
['Sentence 2', 'Sentence 3', 'Sentence 4', 'Sentence 2', 'Sentence 3']
['Sentence 1', 'Sentence 4', 'Sentence 3', 'Sentence 2', 'Sentence 4']
['Sentence 4', 'Sentence 2', 'Sentence 3', 'Sentence 4', 'Sentence 2']
['Sentence 2', 'Sentence 3', 'Sentence 4', 'Sentence 3', 'Sentence 2']
['Sentence 4', 'Sentence 3', 'Sentence 2', 'Sentence 3', 'Sentence 4']
['Sentence 1', 'Sentence 4', 'Sentence 2', 'Sentence 3', 'Sentence 4']
['Sentence 3', 'Sentence 2', 'Sentence 1', 'Sentence 4', 'Sentence 2']
['Sentence 3', 'Sentence 2', 'Sentence 4', 'Sentence 3', 'Sentence 2']
['Sentence 1', 'Sentence 2', 'Sentence 3', 'Sentence 2', 'Sentence 4']
['Sentence 2', 'Sentence 3', 'Sentence 4', 'Sentence 1', 'Sentence 4']
['Sentence 4', 'Sentence 3', 'Sentence 2', 'Sentence 1', 'Sentence 4']
```

FIGURE 4.4: It is paths generated by 2nd order random walk algorithm.

3. **Word2Vec context feature:** In this step, the random walk returns a path consisting of a series of random steps such as [“sentence 4", “sentence 3", “sentence 2", “sentence 1", “sentence 4"]. These sentences are tokenized into tokens and merged in a single list as shown in Fig. 4.6, the list is fed to the Word2Vec model to produce 5-dimensional word embeddings based on the graph to show the small demonstration in Table 4.3. Further, we calculate the mean of the 5-dimensional word embeddings within each sentence to create the Node2Vec features in Table 4.4. These embeddings capture the structural and relational properties of the graph through biased random

walks, which are parameterized by the p and q values to balance exploration and exploitation [5].

Here, Fig. 4.5 shows the generalized demonstration of the article. Where, S_n is the nth sentence in the article A_1 and W_m denotes the total number of words in the article A_1. Which, the controlling parameters are used to train node2vec features as given in the given Table 4.5.

TABLE 4.3: This is the vector representation of each word using Word2Vec

words ⇓	**5-dimensional word embedding**				
and	.56	.46	.36	.26	.16
computer	.50	.40	.30	.20	.10
designed	.52	.42	.32	.22	.12
developed	.51	.41	.31	.21	.11
hardware	.53	.43	.33	.23	.13
has	.54	.44	.34	.24	.14
How	.55	.45	.35	.25	.15
interacts	.57	.47	.37	.27	.17
is	.58	.48	.38	.28	.18
parts	.59	.49	.39	.29	.19
software	.501	.401	.301	.201	.101
system	.511	.411	.311	.211	.111
This	.521	.421	.321	.221	.121
two	.531	.431	.331	.231	.131
well	.541	.441	.341	.241	.141
with	.551	.451	.351	.251	.151

TABLE 4.4: This is the vector representation of each sentence by taking the mean of all word embedding vectors to generate a single vector representing the entire sentence

Sentences ⇓	**5-dimensional sentence embedding**				
This is computer system.	.528	.428	.328	.228	.128
Computer has software and hardware two parts.	.536	.436	.336	.236	.136
How software interacts with hardware.	.5404	.4404	.3404	.2404	.1404
How well software is developed and designed.	.537	.437	.337	.237	.137

[5] the exploration-exploitation tradeoff is a dynamic balancing act between trying new things to learn (exploration) and using existing knowledge to make the best decisions (exploitation). Finding the right balance is crucial for efficient learning and optimization in many domains.

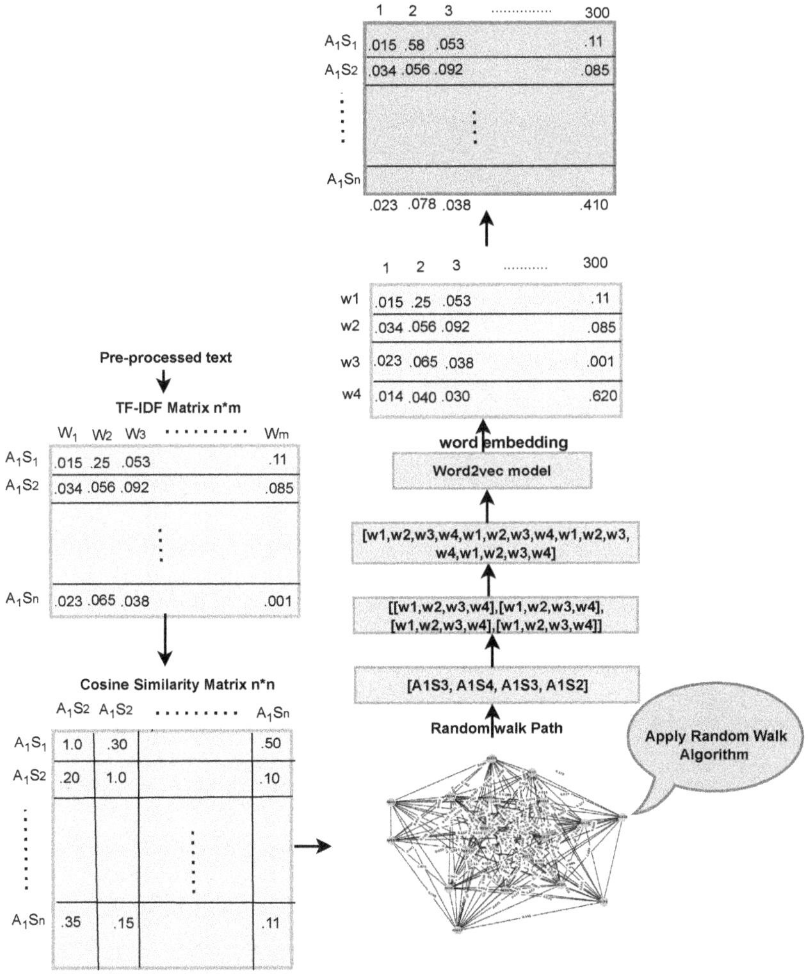

FIGURE 4.5: Procedure for Node2Vec feature

4.2.3 Creating label

In the text summarization task, reference summaries serve as annotations corresponding to the article, but they need to be converted into numerical form to train regression models. To achieve this, we employed Word Mover's Distance (WMD) [134] to map each sentence in the article to each sentence in the reference summary. Specifically, we calculated the similarity between each sentence in the

['sentence 4', 'sentence 3', 'sentence 2', 'sentence 1', 'sentence 4']

['how well software is developed and design', 'how software interacts with hardware', 'computer has software and hardware two parts', 'This is computer system', 'how well software is developed and design',]

[['how', 'well', 'software', 'is', 'developed', 'and', 'design'], ['how', 'software', 'interacts', 'with', 'hardware'], ['computer', 'has', 'software', 'and', 'hardware', 'two', 'parts'], ['this', 'is', 'computer', 'system'], ['how', 'well', 'software', 'is', 'developed', 'and', 'design']]

['how', 'well', 'software', 'is', 'developed', 'and', 'design', 'how', 'software', 'interacts', 'with', 'hardware', 'computer', 'has', 'software', 'and', 'hardware', 'two', 'parts', 'this', 'is', 'computer', 'system', 'how', 'well', 'software', 'is', 'developed', 'and', 'design']

FIGURE 4.6: This is a random walk path converted by the original sentence and fed into Word2Vec to generate context word embedding

document and each sentence in the reference summary using WMD. Then, we defined the similarity of a sentence in the document as the maximum similarity with any sentence in the reference summary, normalized by the maximum similarity of any sentence in the document. This process enables us to represent the reference summary as numerical values, allowing us to train our models to predict summary scores for each sentence in the article.

4.2.4 ML regression models for summarization

The generated embeddings are then used as input features for the ML models. We preprocess the embeddings to ensure compatibility with the model input format. The embeddings are then fed into supervised ML regression models to predict a continuous target variable, summarization scores, based on Node2Vec features as predictor variables. To determine the best regression model for text summarization, we implemented and evaluated eight different models: (1) Support vector regression (SVR); (2) Linear regression (LR); (3) K-neighbors regressor (KNR); (4) Random forest regressor (RFR); (5) Bayesian Ridge (BR); (6) Gradient boosting regressor (GBR); (7) Decision tree regressor (DTR); (8) AdaBoost regressor (ABR).

We evaluated the performance of each regression model using node2vec features for each language. The results of this evaluation are presented in Section 4.4.

4.2.5 Summary generation

The resulting extracted summary is generated in four different lengths: 10%, 20%, 30%, and 40% of the original article. These lengths are determined based on the sentence rankings produced by each ML regression model, which is integrated with the node2vec feature set. In other words, the highest-ranked sentences from each model are selected to construct the summary, with its length ranging from 10% to 40% of the original article.

4.3 Experimental Setup

In this study, we have elaborated on the hyperparameter tuning strategies, training data splits, and evaluation metrics used to assess model performance. So, we evaluate our proposed framework on three different languages datasets under various parameter settings. We utilized various parameter settings to perform a random walk on the graph, including P=4, q=1, number of walks (10, 13, 15), number of steps (50, 100, 100), window size (50), and dimensions for Node2Vec embeddings (200,300,200). Among these configurations, the best results were achieved with the parameters [P=4, q=1, number of walks =13, number of steps = 100, window size = 50, dimensions for Node2Vec embeddings = 300]. We decided on initial values based on values used in the existing literature.

So, we set the parameters to extract the Node2Vec features from these datasets, as specified in Table 4.5. In addition, we compare our results with current state-of-the-art techniques. Specifically, we use different parameters to obtain the feature set from random walks followed by Word2Vec. In the context of random walk algorithms:

- Number of walks refers to the number of times a random walk is initiated from different nodes or the same node within a graph.
- Each walk consists of a fixed number of steps, where the walk moves from the current node to a neighboring node chosen at random.
- The Return Parameter (P) controls the likelihood of immediately revisiting a node in the walk, with higher values resulting in fewer revisits.

- The In-Out Parameter (q) determines the walk's bias, with q=1 indicating an unbiased walk that has an equal probability of visiting any neighboring node.

By tuning these parameters, we can adjust the behavior of the random walk algorithm to extract Node2Vec features that capture different aspects of the graph structure and node relationships.

TABLE 4.5: Controlling parameters setting

Parameters	**value**	Range
Number of walk	13	[10, 13, 15]
Number of step	100	[50, 100, 100]
Return parameter (p)	4	-
In-out parameter (q)	1	-
window_size	50	-
Word2vec dimension	300	[200, 300, 200]
Dimension of node2vec features	300	-

4.4 Results & Discussion

Here, we have analyzed the result obtained from the proposed ML regression model with Node2Vec features set on three benchmark datasets. The corresponding results are shown in Tables 4.6, 4.7, 4.8 and 4.9 at compression rates 40%, 30%, 20%, and 10%, respectively, in all three Hindi, Gujarati, and English datasets.

A higher compression rate typically results in shorter summaries, which may improve conciseness but can also lead to the omission of important contextual or semantic information, potentially reducing coherence, informativeness, and overall summary quality. Conversely, lower compression rates allow for more content to be retained, often leading to more informative and fluent summaries, albeit at the cost of reduced conciseness. In our experiments, we carefully analyzed this trade-off by evaluating multiple compression settings. The results indicate that moderate compression rates provide a balanced compromise, preserving key information while maintaining readability and coherence. These findings suggest that selecting an appropriate compression rate is task- and application-dependent, and our framework is designed to allow flexible adjustment of this parameter to meet different user and application requirements.

The random forest regression (RFR) model performs the best in all performance metrics and for all three datasets. The Random Forest Regressor (RFR) frequently demonstrates superior performance compared to other regression models due to its ensemble-based learning strategy and strong generalization capabilities. By constructing multiple decision trees using bootstrapped samples of the training data and random subsets of features, RFR effectively reduces variance and mitigates overfitting, which are common limitations of single-tree models. Furthermore, RFR is less sensitive to hyperparameter settings compared to models such as Support Vector Regression or Gradient Boosting, making it easier to tune and more consistent across different datasets.

For the Hindi language, the results at 40% compression rate for ROUGE-1, ROUGE-2, and ROUGE-L metrics are 60.6, 42.0, and 52.0, respectively. Similarly, for the Gujarati language, the corresponding results are 47.0, 29.0, and 41.6. The corresponding results for the DUC-2002 dataset are 53.5, 25.5, and 50.5 as shown in Table 4.6. At a compression rate 30% , the results for ROUGE-1, ROUGE-2, and ROUGE-L are 51.7, 32.5, and 43.1 for the Hindi dataset and 39.3, 21.9 and 33.8 for the Gujarati dataset. The corresponding results for the DUC-2002 dataset based on the same set of metrics are 50.0, 21.0, and 48.0 as shown in Table 4.7. At a compression rate 20%, the results are 40.9, 23.4 and 33.8 for ROUGE-1, ROUGE-2 and ROUGE-L scores, respectively, on the Hindi dataset. The same for the Gujarati dataset are 29.5, 14.7, and 25.4. The corresponding results on the DUC-2002 dataset are 47.0, 29.4, and 41.60 based on the same metrics as shown in Table 4.8.

We have evaluated the results at a 40% compression rate, demonstrating the effectiveness of the XSumm_ML-RFR-node2vec model compared to various state-of-the-art (SOTA) techniques, as shown in Table 4.10 for Hindi and Gujarati languages. The SOTA techniques for Hindi and Gujarati languages are: (1) combining the k-means clustering algorithm with the Word2Vec model and autoencoders for extractive summarization in [28]. (2) used the IndicBART multilingual sequence-to-sequence pre-trained model to generate text summaries for Indian languages in [103]. (3) explored the application of pre-trained models for abstractive summarization, specifically using IndicBART and mT5 models in [104]. These models were fine-tuned for the summarization task, demonstrating their effectiveness in generating concise and informative summaries for Indian languages. (4) also used the fine-tuned SOTA PEGASUS model, which performed best for English and

Gujarati, while the fine-tuned IndicBART model with augmented data produced the best results for Hindi. Our proposed model outperforms transformers such as PEGASUS and IndicBART compared to Node2vec integrated with ML models.

On the other hand, the corresponding results on the DUC 2002 dataset are presented in Table 4.11. These results were obtained after implementing the SOTA techniques for the DUC 2002 dataset in the same split ratio as in [7]. For this dataset, our suggested method outperforms state-of-the-art RNN-based summarization techniques, including SummCoder [72], HSSAS [76], CoRank [38] and DeepSumm [48], all of which make use of the documents latent topic information. The other two baselines [7] models depend on statistical and linguistic features and XSumm-PSO [7] is used to optimize the features. In addition, readers find the summaries produced by the system to be coherent and easy to read. ML regression models outperform deep learning models in this specific context. The key reasons include: (1) we used the Hindi, Gujarati, and DUC-2002 datasets to train ML regression models instead of deep learning models, where deep learning models may struggle due to underfitting and the need for extensive training data, as these datasets contain fewer samples, making them unsuitable for training deep learning models. Meanwhile, traditional ML regression models perform better when working with smaller datasets. (2) Another key observation was that the gold standard summaries in these datasets consist of phrases and partial sentences that already exist in the original articles. This was the primary reason for choosing ML regression models over deep learning models, as they are more suitable for ranking sentences in extractive rather than abstractive summarization. The extractive approach achieves higher accuracy than the abstractive approach due to the direct extraction of sentences from the original text.

The generated summaries from the proposed model are evaluated by qualitative and quantitative analysis. A qualitative analysis of the generated summaries would provide valuable insight into the readability and coherence of the generated summaries. To address this, we have incorporated the following: (1) Manual Evaluation: we have conducted a qualitative review of generated summaries, assessing factors such as fluency, coherence, and informativeness by comparing human-written summaries. (2) Example Summaries: we have included representative examples in Figures 4.8, 4.9, and 4.10. These examples show sample-generated summaries for datasets in Hindi, Gujarati, and English, respectively, obtained at a 40% compression rate. The blue text in the generated summary matches the gold standard summary. The ROUGE-1_recall values are 82.4, 97.7, and 1.0, for English, Hindi, and Gujarati languages, respectively. The results suggest that the proposed model can effectively handle multi-lingual summarization tasks, providing high-quality summaries for different languages. These additions provide a more comprehensive assessment of summary quality beyond quantitative metrics.

Based on our study, we found that Node2Vec features represent sentences by considering their "context" within random walks. This approach allows for capturing both local and global structural information for each node in the graph, thereby improving the feature representation so that machine learning models can achieve better predictive performance, particularly in tasks involving graph-structured data.

In our proposed approach, the Random forest regression model integrated with Node2Vec features performed better among these ML models because random forests are known for their high accuracy and robustness, making them suitable for handling large datasets effectively.

4.4.1 Conceptual implications

To expand on the broader theoretical and conceptual implications, considered classical ML models, when combined with features derived from random-walk-based techniques such as Node2Vec, can outperform deep learning-based techniques because the feature engineering provided by Node2Vec reduces the reliance on heavy, task-specific deep architectures. Classical methods like Random Forests require significantly fewer computational resources than deep neural networks. ML Models: Typically have fewer layers and parameters. Algorithms like Random Forests and Logistic Regression are relatively straightforward with fewer mathematical operations. The DL Models are composed of multiple layers (e.g., convolutional, recurrent, or fully connected layers) with millions or even billions of parameters, leading to a higher computational load. Thus, the use of classical methods can be helpful in time-sensitive applications and on hardware-constrained devices. A key finding of our proposed research is that classical machine learning methods, Random Forest regression models in our case, have performed better than deep learning models (which often prove to be state-of-the-art in existing literature). This is important from a theoretical and conceptual perspective because classical methods like Random Forests require significantly fewer computational resources compared to deep neural networks. This was possible by extracting features derived from random-walk-based techniques like Node2Vec and feeding them to a Random Forest regression model. Deep Learning models are often composed of multiple layers (e.g., convolutional, recurrent, or fully connected layers) with millions or even billions of parameters, leading to a higher computational load.

Another key finding from a theoretical and conceptual perspective is the difference in performance on Hindi and Gujarati vs. English datasets. The performance of the DUC-2002 (English) dataset is relatively poor compared to the Hindi and Gujarati datasets (see Tables 4.10 and 4.11). This disparity is primarily due to the smaller number of samples in the DUC-2002 dataset, as illustrated in Table 2.1. Hindi (7000+ samples) and Gujrati (8000+ samples) datasets on the other hand are reasonably populated as shown in Table 2.2. To substantiate this further, we repeated the experiments on 576 randomly selected samples from Hindi and Gujarati datasets. For the Gujarati dataset, the ROUGE-1, ROUGE-2, and ROUGE-L scores are 10.2%, 0.3%, and 8.4%, respectively. Similarly, for the Hindi dataset, the scores are 23.8%, 2.0%, and 18.1% on the same metrics. Thus, it appears that the proposed model is sensitive to the number of samples in a dataset and does not generalize well on fewer samples. This is something that researchers should be aware of while applying the proposed model in the future. This can be attributed to the fact that Hindi is a more complex language in comparison to English. Hindi has 52 characters (vs. 26 characters in the English language) and grammatically has far more variations with respect to gender and number. For example, for the sample English sentence shown in Fig. 4.7, there are six variations in Hindi depending upon the gender, number, and seniority of the person being talked about. Something similar holds for the Gujarati language as well.

English: You are good.

Hindi: तुम अच्छे हो। तू अच्छा है। आप अच्छे हैं। तुम अच्छी हो। तू अच्छी है। आप अच्छी हैं।

FIGURE 4.7: Example of variation of Hindi language as compared English language

4.4.2 Ablation Study

To better understand the feature extraction part's contribution to the proposed model's performance, we conduct ablation studies using our proposed model on Hindi, and Gujarati datasets. Here, we have extracted the features from Node2Vec and Word2Vec techniques separately to show the effectiveness of Node2Vec features from Word2Vec features. These features are integrated with the RFR model of ML separately and generate the summary at a 40% compression rate. Now, we check the performance of each feature for the Hindi language in ROUGE - 1, ROUGE-2, and ROUGE-L metrics. The Node2Vec features outperform the Word2Vec features, achieving 60.6%, 42.0%, and 52.0% for ROUGE-1, ROUGE-2, and ROUGE-L, respectively, compared to 44.9%, 22.1%, and 34.1% achieved by Word2Vec features. For the Gujarati language, Node2Vec features similarly outperform Word2Vec features, demonstrating higher ROUGE-1, ROUGE-2, and ROUGE-L scores. Node2Vec achieves scores of 47.0%, 29.4%, and 41.6%, compared to the Word2Vec scores of 42.5%, 21.5%, and 37.6%. This consistent superiority highlights the effectiveness of Node2Vec's graph-based representation in capturing contextual and structural nuances, even in low-resource languages like Gujarati, and Hindi.

It also enhanced feature representation, unlike traditional graph-based methods, Node2Vec generates dense, continuous feature representations that are more suitable for machine learning and deep learning models, improving downstream performance.

Node2Vec is domain-agnostic and can be applied to any text type, from news articles to scientific papers. Node2Vec features have improved ranking by accurately representing the salience of sentence relative to the document's content. It maps high-dimensional relationships into dense vector embeddings, reducing computational overhead in downstream summarization tasks. In this work, we used the sentence-level graph. In that case, Node2Vec allows tuning the balance between local (neighboring nodes) and global (graph-wide) exploration via its hyperparameters: (a) Breadth-first sampling (p) for local context, (b) depth-first sampling (q) for global context. This flexibility ensures that the embeddings can be tailored to focus on the aspects of the graph most relevant to summarization.

TABLE 4.6: Results on Node2Vec features integrated into ML with 40% compression rate for summary based on ROUGE_recall metric in different three languages.

Metrics	ARR	BRR	DTR	GBR	LR	KRR	SVR	RFR
Hindi (FIRE-2022)								
ROUGE-1	49.2	58.5	56.2	52.9	58.5	58.3	53.4	**60.6**
ROUGE-2	35.2	39.7	37.8	31.8	39.9	39.2	32.6	**42.0**
ROUGE-L	43.4	49.6	47.5	42.8	49.7	49.1	43.3	**52.0**
Gujarati (FIRE-2022)								
ROUGE-1	17.8	44.2	38.5	45.9	44.2	41.7	43.9	**47.0**
ROUGE-2	8.9	26.2	21.5	27.1	26.2	24.0	25.6	**29.4**
ROUGE-L	16.2	38.3	33.0	39.5	38.3	35.9	37.7	**41.6**
English (DUC 2002)								
ROUGE-1	34.5	39.6	35.2	38.9	40.6	39.1	37.4	**53.5**
ROUGE-2	13.5	15.9	13.8	15.0	16.7	16.5	14.0	**25.5**
ROUGE-L	31.7	36.4	32.5	35.7	37.5	36.4	34.5	**50.5**

TABLE 4.7: Results on Node2Vec features integrated into ML with 30% compression rate for summary based on ROUGE_recall metric in different three languages.

Metrics	ARR	BRR	DTR	GBR	LR	KRR	SVR	RFR
Hindi (FIRE-2022)								
ROUGE-1	42.3	48.1	47.1	42.5	48.1	48.1	42.7	**51.7**
ROUGE-2	28.8	29.3	29.0	22.8	29.0	28.8	23.0	**32.5**
ROUGE-L	37.2	39.9	39.2	33.6	39.8	39.7	34.1	**43.1**
Gujarati (FIRE-2022)								
ROUGE-1	16.6	35.1	31.0	37.4	34.9	34.2	**39.3**	**39.3**
ROUGE-2	8.2	19.1	16.4	20.3	18.8	18.6	**21.9**	**21.9**
ROUGE-L	15.1	30.3	26.8	31.9	30.1	29.5	**33.8**	**33.8**
English (DUC 2002)								
ROUGE-1	26.5	29.9	27.0	28.7	29.6	28.0	29.0	**50.0**
ROUGE-2	9.6	10.8	9.9	10.0	10.4	9.9	10.0	**21.0**
ROUGE-L	24.3	27.2	24.9	26.2	27.0	25.8	26.6	**48.0**

4.5 Conclusion

In this study, we have implemented XSumm-ML_RFR, a framework for extractive text summarization, utilizing Node2Vec embeddings as primary features in multiple languages. By incorporating Node2Vec, built on a combination of random walks and Word2Vec, we capture rich contextual information that improves summary quality. Among the various regression models tested, the Random Forest Regressor (RFR) demonstrated the best performance. The summaries were generated at compression rates 40%, 30%, 20% and 10% in three languages, with the

TABLE 4.8: Results on Node2Vec features integrated into ML with 20% compression rate for summary based on ROUGE_recall metric in different three languages.

Metrics	ARR	BRR	DTR	GBR	LR	KRR	SVR	RFR
Hindi (FIRE-2022)								
ROUGE-1	34.4	35.5	35.6	24.0	35.4	36.3	29.8	**40.9**
ROUGE-2	22.0	18.7	19.6	13.5	18.5	18.9	13.7	**23.4**
ROUGE-L	30.2	28.9	29.6	23.3	29.0	29.5	23.8	**33.8**
Gujarati (FIRE-2022)								
ROUGE-1	17.5	25.4	23.2	27.4	25.3	26.0	29.5	**29.5**
ROUGE-2	7.2	12.8	11.3	13.5	12.5	13.3	**14.7**	**14.7**
ROUGE-L	13.8	22.1	20.4	23.7	22.0	22.8	**25.4**	**25.4**
English (DUC 2002)								
ROUGE-1	20.3	21.4	19.6	20.3	20.9	19.7	21.7	**47.0**
ROUGE-2	6.8	6.8	6.5	6.1	6.1	6.2	6.7	**29.4**
ROUGE-L	18.5	19.2	18.1	18.4	18.8	18.0	19.8	**41.6**

TABLE 4.9: Results on Node2Vec features integrated into ML with 10% compression rate for summary based on ROUGE_recall metric in different three languages.

Metrics	ARR	BRR	DTR	GBR	LR	KRR	SVR	RFR
Hindi (FIRE-2022)								
ROUGE-1	24.75	16.35	18.55	12.20	16.40	18.70	12.40	21.25
ROUGE-2	16.20	6.60	8.95	4.30	6.55	7.95	4.25	10.05
ROUGE-L	22.40	13.45	15.85	10.10	13.45	15.30	10.20	17.60
Gujarati (FIRE-2022)								
ROUGE-1	12.20	12.00	12.80	14.10	11.90	14.10	14.10	16.00
ROUGE-2	5.60	4.80	5.40	6.10	4.70	6.50	6.10	6.70
ROUGE-L	11.20	10.70	11.60	12.60	10.60	12.80	12.60	14.30
English (DUC 2002)								
ROUGE-1	13.90	14.90	14.70	13.30	15.10	13.80	14.20	23.50
ROUGE-2	2.70	3.20	3.90	3.30	3.30	3.50	3.10	14.70
ROUGE-L	12.60	13.40	13.50	12.20	13.60	12.70	12.80	20.80

effectiveness confirmed by ROUGE-1, ROUGE-2 and ROUGE-L scores detailed in Tables 4.6, 4.7, 4.8, and 4.9. The limitations of Node2Vec features, such as if the underlying graph is large, then many random walks are required, making the approach computationally expensive in terms of time and memory and the efficiency depends on walk length, number of walks, and graph size. Poor parameter tuning p and q in the Node2Vec technique can lead to biased or inefficient embeddings. Standard ML models (e.g. SVMs, Random Forest) may not scale well to very large graphs.

TABLE 4.10: Comparison analysis of proposed XSumm-ML_RFR-Node2Vec model at 40% with other state-of-the-art techniques on Hindi and Gujarati datasets

Datasets ⇒	Hindi (FIRE-2022)		Gujarati (FIRE-2022)	
Methods ⇓	ROUGE-1	ROUGE-2	ROUGE-1	ROUGE-2
IIIT_Ranchi [28]	32.7	17.4	17.6	08.5
SSNCSENLP [135]	37.9	22.5	-	-
PICT CL Lab 2 [103]	54.4	44.3	-	-
Next Gen NLP [102]	55.6	45.5	20.9	11.9
HakunaMatata [104]	59.2	49.2	24.3	14.6
XSumm_ML-RFR-Node2vec	**60.6**	42.0	**47.0**	**29.4**

TABLE 4.11: Comparison analysis of proposed XSumm-ML_RFR-Node2Vec model at 40% with other state-of-the-art techniques on DUC 2002 dataset

Methods	ROUGE-1	ROUGE-2	ROUGE-L
Summcoder [72]	49.0	23.5	40.6
HSSAS [76]	50.5	24.5	42.8
CoRank [38]	51.6	25.8	-
DeepSumm [48]	52.2	25.7	44.2
XSumm-PSO [7]	50.9	22.5	48.5
XSumm_ML-RFR-Node2vec	**53.5**	**25.5**	**50.5**

Generated summary 40% R1-recall 0.977
बिबकोल यानि भारत इम्यूनोजिकल एंड बायोलॉजिकल लिमिटेड (BIBCOL) भारत सरकार की ही कंपनी है और अभी तक यह देश में पोलियो वैक्सीन का उत्पादन करती है |लेकिन देश में इस समय कोरोना वैक्सीन की सबसे ज्यादा जरूरत समझी जा रही है, ऐसे में BIBCOL को कोरोना वैक्सीन का उत्पादन करने के लिए कहा गया है | **एक सूत्र ने कहा कि कंपनी के आवेदन पर विस्तृत विचार-विमर्श के बाद समिति ने प्रस्तावित दूसरे/तीसरे चरण के परीक्षण की अनुमति दिए जाने की सिफारिश की उन्होंने बताया कि यह परीक्षण दिल्ली एवं पटना के एम्स और नागपुर स्थित मेडिट्रिना चिकित्सा विज्ञान संस्थान समेत विभिन्न स्थानों पर किया जाएगा यानि इस कंपनी के पास वैक्सीन उत्पादन की बड़ी क्षमता है|**
Gold summary
बिबकोल यानि भारत इम्यूनोजिकल एंड बायोलॉजिकल लिमिटेड (BIBCOL) भारत सरकार की ही कंपनी है और अभी तक यह देश में पोलियो वैक्सीन का उत्पादन करती है। लेकिन देश में इस समय कोरोना वैक्सीन की सबसे ज्यादा जरूरत समझी जा रही है, ऐसे में BIBCOL को कोरोना वैक्सीन का उत्पादन करने के लिए कहा गया है।

FIGURE 4.8: Generated summary from XSumm-ML_RFR-Node2Vec for Hindi text.

Generated summary 40 % R1-recall 1.0
તે માટે દર્દી અથવા તો તેમના પરિવારજનોએ સેન્ટરના નંબર 63588 45684 પર કોલ કરવાનો રહેશે દાખલ થનાર દર્દીને રહેવા, જમવા તેમજ દવા બાબતે એક પણ રૂપિયો તેમણે અથવા તો તેમના પરિવારજનોએ ચૂકવવાનો રહેશે નહીં. રાજકોટ શહેર અને જિલ્લામાં બની ચૂકેલા કોવિડ કેર સેન્ટરને ટક્કર મારે તે પ્રકારનું કોવિડ સેન્ટર એસ એન કે સ્કૂલ ખાતે બનાવવામાં આવ્યું છે. અહીં ઓક્સિજન બેડ ઉપલબ્ધ કરવામાં આવ્યા છે સેન્ટર દ્વારા એડમિશન પ્રક્રિયામાં પારદર્શિતા રાખવામાં આવશેસી કંપનીના માલિક પરાક્રમસિંહ જાડેજા સહિતના અગ્રણીઓ એક સાથે એક પ્લેટફોર્મ પર આવીને રાજકોટ શહેરમાં એવા પ્રકારનું કોવિડ કેર સેન્ટર શરૂ કર્યું છે સેન્ટરની તમામ સારવાર અને મેડિકલને લગતી બાબતો માટે HCG ગ્રુપ સાથે જોડાણ કરવામાં આવ્યું છે સેન્ટર દ્વારા જાહેર કરવામાં આવેલી પ્રેસ નોટમાં સ્પષ્ટ ઉલ્લેખ કરવામાં આવ્યો છે કે, અહીં કોઇ પણ જાતનું વેઇટીંગ લીસ્ટ રાખવામાં આવશે નહીં દર્દીને કઇ રીતે દાખલ કરી શકાશે?: કોવિડ કેર સેન્ટરની શરૂઆત 50 બેડથી કરવામાં આવશેકે સ્કૂલ (SNK School)માં બનાવવામાં આવેલા કોવિડ કેર સેન્ટર (Covid care centre) માં દર્દીઓને દાખલ કરવામાં આવશે.
Gold summary
રાજકોટ શહેર અને જિલ્લામાં બની ચૂકેલા કોવિડ કેર સેન્ટરને ટક્કર મારે તે પ્રકારનું કોવિડ સેન્ટર એસ એન કે સ્કૂલ ખાતે બનાવવામાં આવ્યું છે.

FIGURE 4.9: Generated summary from XSumm-ML_RFR-Node2Vec for Gujarati text.

Generated summary 40% R1-recall 0.824
The government today imposed direct federal rule in Kashmir, where Indian security forces are battling to put down a rebellion by Moslem separatists., The action follows the killing Tuesday of at least 29 Moslem militants by Indian security forces., In the Pakistani capital of Islamabad, meanwhile, India and Pakistan opened negotiations today aimed at repairing relations threatened by the rebellion in the disputed northern region., Relations between Pakistan and India worsened in January when Indian soldiers cracked down on Moslem militants in Kashmir who are seeking independence from India or union with Pakistan., At least 792 people have been killed in Kashmir since then., India has accused Pakistan of arming and training the militants, a charge Pakistan has denied., Before direct federal rule was imposed today on Jammu-Kashmir state, it was administered temporarily by a governor, a federal representative, since Jan. 18., The announcement of federal rule reflected the belief that Jammu-Kashmir state was too unstable to be run by an elected local government., On Tuesday, at least 29 militants were killed by Indian security forces in Kashmir, the Moslem-dominated northern part of Jammu-Kashmir state and the center of the secessionist campaign., Officials, who cannot be identified under briefing rules, said 21 militants were killed in a battle with the Border Security Force in Poonch, 400 miles northwest of New Delhi., Hours later in the same area, troops killed eight militants who slipped across the border from Pakistan, said the officials., The guards also arrested four militants and seized 14 automatic rifles, two machine guns and two rocket launchers, the officials said., Indian officials maintain that Kashmiri militants regularly cross over to Pakistan through the border and return by the same route after receiving arms training., Pakistan denies it is training or helping the militants, but calls the separatist struggle a fight for self-determination., India and Pakistan have fought two previous wars over Kashmir, in 1948 and 1965., Both were won by India., "About 65 percent of Jammu-Kashmir's 6 million people are Moslems, making it India's only Moslem majority state.
Gold summary
The Indian government imposed direct federal rule in Kashmir where their security forces are battling to put down rebellion by Moslem separatists., This action follows the killing of at least 29 Moslem militants by Indian security forces., Meanwhile, in the Pakistani capital Islamabad, Pakistan and India began negotiations to repair deteriorating conditions between the two countries., India claims, and Pakistan denies, that Kashmiri militants cross into Pakistan for arms and training., The announcement of federal rule was made in the belief that the state was too unstable for elected government., Since India cracked down on the militants, 792 people have been killed.

FIGURE 4.10: Generated summary from XSumm-ML_RFR-Node2Vec for English text.

Chapter 5

Feature-Based Extractive Summarization of Indian Language Documents

The objectives of this chapter are following[1]:

- To introduce extractive summarization for multiple Indian languages using statistical and linguistic features.
- To discuss the importance of each feature extracted for each sentence in the article.
- To examine the proposed model with different seven Indian languages named: Telugu, Tamil, Kannad, Hindi, English, Gujgarati and Bengali.

5.1 Introduction

The field of natural language processing (NLP) has shown limited focus on automatic text summarization for indian languages. Unlike languages such as English, Chinese, French, and German, Indian languages lack large-scale datasets. Most existing datasets are either inaccessible to the public or too small for practical use. To address this gap, the forum for information retrieval evaluation (FIRE)[10] [2] has

[1] The content of this chapter is based on [[8], [Accepted]]
[2] http://fire.irsi.res.in/fire/register

taken a significant step by creating reusable corpora for indian language summarization through a collaborative effort. This initiative provides datasets in three major Indian languages at ILSUM-2022 track [3]: Hindi, English, and Gujarati. Next, they included one another language named: Bengali with the ILSUM-2022 track in ILSUM-2023 tarck. They also provided datasets in seven major Indian languages for this task at ILSUM-2024: Hindi, Indian English, Gujarati, Tamil, Telugu, Kannada and Bengali.

The FIRE hosted a competition task for Indian Language Summarization (ILSUM), in which the dataset consists of articles and headline pairs from several of the country's most prominent newspapers. The task for each article is to write a meaningful fixed-length summary, either extractive or abstractive.

This chapter focuses on Indian languages extractive summarization techniques specifically designed for single document. Two approaches have been proposed named: XSumm-Ten_AF and Sangita_NIT_Patna team to identify summaries for Indian languages. The detailed description of the XSumm-Ten_AF is mention under the section 5.2. The detailed description of the Sangita_NIT_Patna team is mention under the section 5.3. In both proposed approaches, there is no concept of training and testing. In this appproach, We haved just extracted the features and based upon these features to create a summary for each Indian languages.

5.2 Extractive Summarization of two Indian Languages based on statistical and linguistic features

The first approach proposes XSumm-Ten_AF approach that works on two Indian languages (Hindi and English), as provided by the organizers of ILSUM-2022 for extractive approach. The linguistic features used in the XSum-TenAF model did not require extensive language-specific adaptations or specialized, language-dependent dictionaries for Indian languages. Instead, the features were designed to remain largely language-agnostic, relying on generalizable statistical properties. We employed ten statistical and linguistic features such as Sentence Position , Sentence Length , sentence numeric , sentence thematic , sentence entropy , part

[3]http://fire.irsi.res.in/fire/2022/home

of speech (noun and verb), TF-ISF (term frequency-inverse document frequency), sentence aggregation , busy path , title match for the extractive summaries from the English and Hindi languages.

The remaining of the paper is formatted as follows. Section 5.2.1 presents our proposed framework. Section 5.2.2 presents the results of this approach. Section 5.2.3 presents conclusion of the proposed framework.

5.2.1 Proposed Model

In this work, we proposed XSumm-TenAF method for extractive Hindi and English summarization. The proposed model used ten hand craft features having statistical and linguistic information. The proposed model produces multi-sentence summaries, with the overall architecture depicted in Figure 5.1.

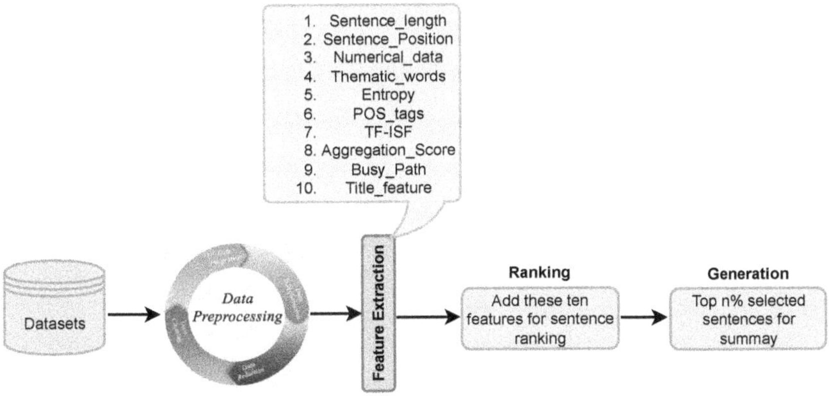

FIGURE 5.1: Flow diagram of the XSumm-TenAF method for extractive summarization task.

5.2.1.1 Problem Assertion

Our goal is to generate concise and relevant summaries (descriptors) that capture the essence of extensive text collections consisting of articles. Consider the following: the input sequence of article with sentences $S_1, S_2, ..., S_N$, and the generated output sequence is $y_1, y_2...., y_n$ similar to article in meaning, $n < N$ – indicating that n is the no. of sentences for generated summary where, N is the no. of sentences for article.

5.2.1.2 Data Preprocessing

Data pre-processing refers to the initial phase of data preparation, where raw data is cleaned, transformed, and organized to enhance its quality and make it suitable for analysis. After pre-processing, cleaned text corpus has been obtained.

- **Sentence tokenization:-** The input article is split into individual sentences using the (|, .) as the delimiter for Hindi and English languages, respectively.
- **Word tokenization:-** Word tokenization involves dividing a text into separate words or tokens, utilizing the space delimiter for both Hindi and English languages.
  First, in pre-processing step, remove null and duplicates values from the both datasets, then sentence and word tokenization are employed in both languages.
- **Punctuation removal:-** Unwanted symbol like this [.,′, ?, !, ; , :, ” ”, (), [], – ..., /, ;̂∗, &, _] are removed from the text.
- **Stop word removal:-** Stop word removal involves eliminating common words that are considered to be of little value in representing the meaning of a text. These words, known as stop words, typically include frequently occurring words such as “the", “and", “is", and other common words that don’t contribute much to the overall meaning of the text.
  Punctuation and stop words removal techniques are used in only English language.

5.2.1.3 Features extraction

For each pre-processed document, ten features are extracted for every sentence, which are described below. For convenience of notation, each feature is subscripted with ij indexing denoting the jth sentence in the ith document. A combined feature set for the jth sentence in the Dth document is represented by a 10-dimensional vector $f_{Dj} = \{f^1_{Dj}, f^2_{Dj}, \ldots, f^{10}_{dj}\}$.

1. **Sentence Position (SP_{Dj}) :-** The article is having N number of sentences. The sentences assigned higher scores (closer to 1) to sentences positioned in the beginning or end of the article and lower scores (closer to 0) to sentences

positioned near the middle of the article. Then sentence position of each sentence is calculated using equation 5.1.

$$SP_{Dj} = \frac{|N/2 - j|}{N/2} \tag{5.1}$$

where, j is the sentence number.

2. **Sentence Length** (SL_{Dj}) **:-** The article is having N number of sentences. Short sentences are having lack of information and lengthy sentences are massive. That's why sentences are considered as important in term of average length sentences. So first determines the maximum (maxL) and minimum (minL) sentence lengths then calculate the average sentence length (Mean) using equation 5.2. Then average sentence length of each sentence is calculated using equation 5.3.

$$Mean = \frac{maxL + MinL}{2} \tag{5.2}$$

$$SL_{Dj} = \frac{1 - |Mean - L_j|}{MaxL} \tag{5.3}$$

Calculate a score for each sentence based on its deviation from the average sentence length. L_j refers to j^{th} sentence length.

3. **Sentence Numeric** (SN_{Dj}) **:-** The article is having N number of sentences. If sentence is having some numeric values, it means, that is important. Then sentence numeric of each sentence is calculated using equation 5.4.

$$SN_{Dj} = \frac{CountN_j}{MaxCountN_D} \tag{5.4}$$

The $countN_j$ is representing the number of numeric values in j^{th} sentence. The $MaxCountN_D$ is assigned the largest numric values of any sentence in the article.

4. **Sentence Thematic** (ST_{Dj}) **:-** In this feature, the top 50% of high-frequency words in an article are considered to score the sentences. This feature compares each word in each sentence of the article with top 50% of high-frequency words in an article, counting the words for each sentence. The scores undergo normalization through division by their maximum value.

5. **Sentence Entropy** (SE_{Dj}) **:-** In this feature, firstly, the probability distribution of each sentence in article is calculated. The calculated probability distribution is utilized to calculate the entropy of the sentence. The equation 5.5 for entropy is given below.

$$SE_{Dj} = \sum_{w \in T}^{j} -(p(w) * log_2(p(w))) \tag{5.5}$$

   where, j stands for the jth sentence in the Dth document, while $p(w)$ denotes the probability of a word (w) in the document (D). T is the collection of words in the sentence.

6. **PosTag** (NV_{Dj})**:-**The feature utilizes the Natural Language Toolkit (NLTK) for part-of-speech tagging. It counts the occurrences of specific part-of-speech tags such as NN, NNC, JVB, VNN, NNP, NVB, VFM, VAUX in each sentence in document. The counts are normalized by dividing them with the maximum count of any sentence in the document.

7. **TF-ISF** (TI_{Dj})**:-**The TF-ISF (Term Frequency-Inverse Sentence Frequency) formula is a measure used to assess the importance of a word in a specific sentence within a larger corpus. It combines the concepts of term frequency TF and ISF.

$$TF\text{-}ISF(w, s, D) = TF(w, s) * ISF(w, D) \tag{5.6}$$

   where: w is the word, s is the sentence, D is the entire document or corpus.

   The TF-ISF score combines the local importance of a term (w) within a sentence (TF) with its global uniqueness across the document or corpus (ISF).

$$TF(w, s) = \frac{\#\text{Times w appears in sentence}}{\#\text{ Total words in sentence s}} \tag{5.7}$$

   This quantifies the frequency of a term appearing within a given sentence in relation to the total number of terms present in that sentence

$$ISF(w, D) = log_2 \frac{\#\text{Total sentences in D}}{\#\text{sentences containing word w}} \tag{5.8}$$

   This measures how unique a term is across all sentences in the document or corpus. The logarithmic scaling is often used to give more weight to terms that occur in fewer sentences.

$$TI_{Dj} = \sum_{w \in T}^{j} TF\text{-}ISF(w, s, D) \tag{5.9}$$

where, j stands for the jth sentence in the Dth document, while $TF\text{-}ISF(w, s, D)$ denotes the probability of a word (w) in the sentence. T stands for the collection of words in the sentence.

8. **Sentence Aggregation** (SA_{Dj}) **:-** This feature captures the similarity of a sentence with respect to the remaining sentences in the document. For the Dth document, let V_i denote its vocabulary. Then, the jth sentence in the Dth document is represented as a vector of size $|V_i|$ having an entry corresponding to each term $t \in V_i$. For a term $t \in V_i$, the corresponding entry in the document vector is the TF-ISF value for w computed as per Eq. 6. The similarity between two sentences is computed as the cosine similarity between their corresponding vectors. The aggregation score (SA_{Dj}) feature value for the jth sentence in the Dth document is defined in equation 5.10 as the aggregation (sum) of the similarity scores of the sentence computed with the remaining sentences in the document.

$$SA_{Dj} = \sum_{\substack{k=1 \\ k \neq j}}^{N_D} \text{Sim}(s_{Dj}, s_{Dk}) \tag{5.10}$$

where N_D denotes the total number of sentences in the Dth document.

9. **Busy Path** (BP_{Dj}) **:-** This feature is calculated using cosine similarity scores between two sentences their corresponding vectors such as TF-IDF as mentioned in above feature 8. The similarity scores are converted to binary values using a threshold of 0.7 as shown in equation 5.11. If a similarity score is greater than 0.7, it is assigned a value of 0; otherwise, it is assigned a value of 1. Then count zero similarity score of each sentence as given in equation 5.12 are normalized by dividing them with the maximum score using equation 5.13.

$$B_{jk} = \begin{cases} 0, & \text{if } \text{Sim}(s_{Dj}, s_{Dk}) > 0.7 \\ 1, & \text{otherwise} \end{cases} \tag{5.11}$$

where B_{jk} denotes the binary similarity indicator between sentences S_{jD} and S_{kD}. For each sentence S_{Dj}, the number of zero-valued similarity indicators is computed as:

$$Z_{Dj} = \sum_{\substack{k=1 \\ k \neq j}}^{N_D} \mathbb{I}(B_{jk} = 0) \tag{5.12}$$

where $\mathbb{I}(\cdot)$ is the indicator function.

$$BP_{Dj} = \frac{Z_{Dj}}{\max_{j}(Z_{Dj})} \tag{5.13}$$

10. **Title Match (TM_{Dj}) :-** This feature compares each word in each sentence of the article with the words in the heading, counting the matches for each sentence. The matching scores are normalized by dividing them with the maximum score.

5.2.1.4 Ranking

In this section, we rank the sentences based on ten handcrafted features. Each sentence in the document has these ten features, which are used to determine its ranking by addition such as $R_{Dj} = \{f^1_{Dj} + f^2_{Dj}+, ..., +f^{10}_{Dj}\}$.

5.2.1.5 Summary Generation

Here, we select top $n\%$ sentences to produce the extractive text summaries based uopn its ranking.

5.2.2 Results

In this section, we analysis the obtained results from the proposed framework on datasets provided by ILSUM-2022 (detalis of the datasets is mentioned under the sub-section 2.2.2.1). Tables 5.1 and 5.2 shown the results produced by XSumm-TenAF model for English and Hindi languages at $n\%$ compression rate, respectively, specifically focusing on ROUGE-1 (R-1), ROUGE-2 (R-2), and ROUGE-L (R-L) metrics in terms of precision (p), recall (r), and F1 scores (details of this metrics are mentioned in section 2.1). Notably, Rouge metrics prioritize recall, leading us to emphasize the evaluation of model performance based on this metric. The XSumm-TenAF demonstrates superior performance at 20% compression rate compared to other state-of-the-art (SOTA) methods in Table 5.3, particularly when evaluated results based on the recall metric for both English and Hindi languages. Kumari et al. [28] employed K-means clustering with combination of word2vec and autoencoder for extractive text summarization in Hindi, English and Gujarati languages. Singh et al. [6] designed enocder decoder and sequence to sequence model for Hindi and English languages. Kumar et al. [14] used genetic algorithm with statistical features to generate tthe extractive summary. Agarwal et al. [103] employed IndicBART for abstractive text summary in Hindi language.

TABLE 5.1: Performance of the proposed XSumm-TenAF model on the FIRE-2022 (ILSUM) English dataset at different compression rates.

Metrics	XSumm-TenAF-20%	XSumm-TenAF-15%	XSumm-TenAF-10%
$R\text{-}1_r$	48.33	34.68	21.69
$R\text{-}1_p$	13.23	10.82	7.63
$R\text{-}1_{f1}$	19.40	15.37	10.60
$R\text{-}2_r$	34.83	23.54	13.88
$R\text{-}2_p$	7.77	6.24	4.28
$R\text{-}2_{f1}$	11.71	9.05	6.06
$R\text{-L}_r$	45.72	10.08	20.03
$R\text{-L}_p$	12.50	32.41	7.03
$R\text{-L}_{f1}$	45.72	32.41	20.03

TABLE 5.2: Performance of the proposed XSumm-TenAF model on the FIRE-2022 (ILSUM) Hindi dataset at different compression rates.

Metrics	XSumm-TenAF-20%	XSumm-TenAF-15%	XSumm-TenAF-10%
$R\text{-}1_r$	59.84	49.07	36.05
$R\text{-}1_p$	29.90	30.04	27.55
$R\text{-}1_{f1}$	37.86	35.52	29.79
$R\text{-}2_r$	43.67	32.95	17.06
$R\text{-}2_p$	19.58	19.33	22.15
$R\text{-}2_{f1}$	25.25	22.69	18.20
$R\text{-L}_r$	53.04	42.75	30.93
$R\text{-L}_p$	26.63	26.66	23.92
$R\text{-L}_{f1}$	53.04	42.75	30.93

5.2.3 Conclusion

We developed effective XSumm-TenAF framework to create extractive text summarizers, achieving success in both Hindi and English summarization tasks. Framework is built on the ten hand crafted features by using statistical and linguistic

TABLE 5.3: Comparison analysis of proposed XSumm-TenAF model at 20% with other state-of-the-art techniques on Hindi and English datasets

Datasets ⇒	Hindi (FIRE-2022)			English (FIRE-2022)		
Methods ⇓	R-1	R-2	R-L	R-1	R-2	R-L
ILSUM-2022 [6]	23.89	-	-	32.83	16.58	-
SUMIL22 [14]	-	-	-	38.44	25.84	-
IIIT-Ranchi [28]	32.72	17.39	-	32.09	18.61	
IndicBART [103]	54.43	44.32	-			-
XSumm-TenAF-20%	**59.84**	**43.67**	**53.04**	**48.33**	**34.83**	**45.72**

features. Thorough evaluation conducted on the ILSUM-2022 datasets (comprising both English and Hindi data) shows that the XSumm-TenAF produce noteworthy results in Tables 5.1 and 5.2 at 10%, 15% and 20% compression rate.

5.3 Extractive Summarization of five Indian Languages based on TF-IDF and SVD

The second approach developed a extractive text summarization framework for a single document using TF-IDF and SVD techniques for seven Indian languages (Bengali, Hindi, Gujarati, Tamil and Telugu, Kannada, English) provided by the organisers of ILSUM-2024 [136].

The remaining of the paper is formatted as follows. Section 5.3.1 presents our proposed framework. Section 5.3.2 presents the results and discussion of this approach. Section 5.3.3 presents conclusion of the proposed framework.

5.3.1 Proposed method

In this section, we proposed an extractive text summarization framework for varioues Indian languagess. We will explain each step in detail in the following section, and the overall architecture is shown in Figure 5.2. So, the proposed model generates multi-sentence summaries.

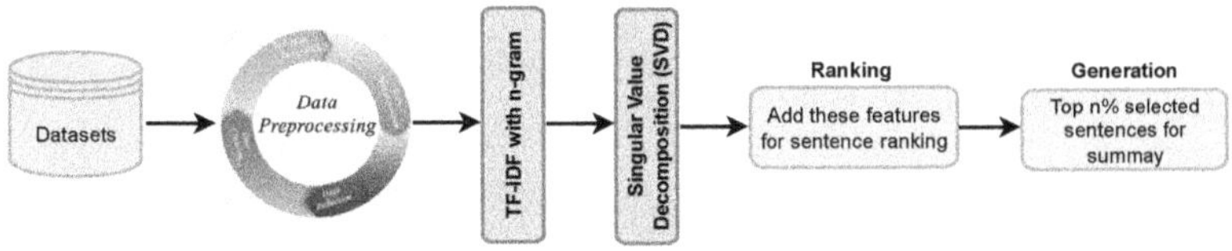

FIGURE 5.2: Architecture for extractive text summarization across multiple languages

5.3.1.1 Data Preprocessing

We preprocessed the dataset by removing the missing and duplicates values from the "Article" or "Summary" columns. We then tokenized the article into sentences and removed punctuation and empty strings to prepare the text for further processing.

5.3.1.2 TF-IDF with n-gram

In this section, we used TF-IDF technique to respresent the sentence in the vector form of the article. Here, the TF-IDF vectorizer is configured to extract features from the text data using a range of n-grams, including single words (unigrams), two-word combinations (bigrams), three-word combinations (trigrams), and four-word combinations (4-grams). By selecting the top 2000 most frequent terms across all documents, the TF-IDF matrix is truncated, reducing its dimensionality and focusing on the most important terms. This helps conserve memory and boost computational efficiency. It combines two measures:

1. **Term Frequency (TF)**: Term Frequency (TF) is a numerical measure that represents how frequently a term appears in a given document. Here, t represents a word (or n-gram, which could be a single word or a sequence of n words), and d represents a specific document. This score increases with the frequency of a word in a document but doesn't consider whether the word is common across other documents in the corpus. The TF score indicates the relative importance of a term within a document by measuring its occurrence. For a specific n-gram g in a document d, the TF is calculated as:

$$\mathrm{TF}(t, d) = \frac{f_{t,d}}{\sum_{t' \in G} f_{t',d}} \tag{5.14}$$

where

- $f_{t,d}$ is the frequency of n-gram t in the document d.
- G is the set of all n-grams in the document d.
- $\sum_{t' \in G} f_{t',d}$ is the total count of all n-grams in the document.

2. **Inverse Document Frequency (IDF)**: Measures how common or rare a word is across all documents in the corpus. A word that appears in many documents will have a lower IDF score. If a term appears in almost every document, its IDF score will be close to zero, meaning it has less unique significance. The inverse document frequency of n-gram t is:

$$\mathrm{IDF}(t) = \log\left(\frac{N}{1 + n_t}\right) \tag{5.15}$$

where, N is the total number of documents in the corpus, n_t is the number of documents containing the n-gram t.

3. **TF-IDF Calculation:** The TF-IDF score for a term in a document is the product of its TF and IDF scores:

$$TF\text{-}IDF(t, d) = \mathrm{TF}(t, d) \times \mathrm{IDF}(t) \tag{5.16}$$

Words with high TF-IDF scores are considered important or unique to that document compared to other documents in the corpus.

5.3.1.3 Singular value decomposition (SVD):

SVD is a mathematical technique used in linear algebra for decomposing a matrix into three other matrices. SVD is used in Latent Semantic Analysis (LSA) to uncover relationships between terms and documents by reducing dimensionality in text data. SVD can reduce the dimensionality of feature vectors for sentences in the article, produced by the TF-IDF technique, while preserving the essential features and relationships in the article.

$$A = U \sum V^T \tag{5.17}$$

- A is a matrix of dimension M× N.
- U: $M \times M$ matrix of the orthonormal eigenvectors of AA^T.
- $\sum$: diagonal matrix with r elements equal to the root of the positive eigenvalues of AA^T or $A^T A$.
- V^T: transpose of a $N \times N$ matrix containing the orthonormal eigenvectors of $A^T A$.

The sums the rows of V^T, giving a score for each sentence based on its importance.

5.3.1.4 Ranking

In this step, we prioritize the sentences in the article, ranking them in descending order of importance. This produces a list of ranked sentences, with the most important sentences at the top and the less significant ones at the bottom.

5.3.1.5 Generation

To generate the summary, we first calculate the sentence count by taking n=15% of the total sentences. We then combine the top-ranked sentences up to this count to create the summary.

5.3.2 Results & Discussion

In this section, to evaluate the our model, we utilized the ILSUM-2024 datasets provided by FIRE-2024 [136] as mention in Table 2.3 in chapter 2. We discussed about the results obtained on Training, validation and test datasets provided by ILSUM-2024 [137] [9]. Table 5.4 shows the results on the training dataset for all different languages for Task 1. Table 5.5 shows the results on the validation dataset for five different languages for Task 1. The corresponding results for the test datasets are presented in tables range from 5.6 and 5.10. In the Hindi and Telugu languages category, we secured the 4th position and present the corresponding results in Table 5.7 and Table 5.10, respectively, for Task 1. Similarly, for the Tamil language, we achieved the 5th position and show the results in Table 5.9. In the Bengali and Gujarati languages category, we secured the 3rd position and present the corresponding results in Table 5.6 and Table 5.8, respectively, for Task 1. In this study, TF-IDF was employed to represent text data by assigning weights to terms based on their importance within the corpus. With respect to the selection of n-gram ranges, our choice was guided by a balance between capturing sufficient contextual information and controlling feature dimensionality and sparsity. Specifically, we selected the n-gram range, including single words (unigrams), two-word combinations (bigrams), three-word combinations (trigrams), and four-word combinations (4-grams) based on preliminary experiments, which indicate that incorporating both unigrams and higher-order n-grams can improve the representation of local context while avoiding excessive noise and computational overhead. This method proved effective in reducing the influence of high-frequency, low-relevance terms, resulting in a more meaningful feature space. Singular value decomposition further enhanced the feature set by capturing latent semantic relationships and reducing dimensionality, thereby improving computational efficiency and model generalization.

Following standard practices in DUC and TAC evaluation settings, which employ strict summary length constraints corresponding to compression ratios of approximately 10-20%, we adopt a 15% summary length to enable fair comparison with prior work. In addition, pilot experiments indicated that this setting provides a suitable balance between conciseness and information retention across the evaluated datasets.

TABLE 5.4: Results on the training dataset for various Indian languages using the proposed approach

Methods	**R-1**			**R-2**			**R-L**		
	Pre	**Rec**	**F1**	**Pre**	**Rec**	**F1**	**Pre**	**Rec**	**F1**
Telugu	17.67	23.47	18.95	10.36	13.70	10.96	17.35	22.92	18.60
Tamil	12.70	17.58	13.53	6.91	9.62	7.27	12.23	16.93	13.01
Kannada	17.27	24.94	19.25	9.93	14.68	11.03	16.82	24.61	18.74
Hindi	29.55	36.00	30.15	13.56	16.57	13.56	27.14	32.97	27.64
English	17.26	36.01	21.51	7.34	16.08	9.12	15.17	31.76	18.92
Gujarati	20.36	27.03	21.70	10.28	13.85	10.87	18.78	24.92	20.00
Bengali	13.74	17.16	13.87	8.12	10.21	8.07	12.34	15.29	12.40

TABLE 5.5: Results on the validation dataset for various Indian languages using the proposed approach

Methods	R-1			R-2			R-L		
	Pre	Rec	F1	Pre	Rec	F1	Pre	Rec	F1
Telugu	17.02	23.54	18.64	9.87	13.68	10.68	16.37	22.61	17.92
Tamil	14.21	19.31	15.08	8.07	11.67	8.75	13.66	18.59	14.51
Kannada	17.63	25.59	19.64	10.13	15.28	11.32	16.75	24.30	18.65
Hindi	28.51	35.74	29.44	12.06	15.88	12.49	24.50	31.04	25.39
English	17.60	36.61	21.93	7.62	16.93	9.51	15.34	32.10	19.13

TABLE 5.6: Results on the testing dataset for Bengali language using the proposed approach

Rank	Team_Name	R-1	R-2	R-4	R-L	B-Pre	B-Rec	B-F1
1	Data Lovers	24.71	16.58	11.87	22.97	73.72	73.16	73.38
2	Curious Coders	24.11	16.10	11.33	22.33	73.84	72.51	73.10
3	NIT_Patna	20.96	14.09	10.57	18.47	69.96	72.33	70.99
4	SynopSizers	19.57	12.24	09.38	16.93	67.55	73.20	70.14
5	SCaLAR	3.97	1.03	00.1	03.79	41.78	60.81	49.48

TABLE 5.7: Results on the testing dataset for Hindi language using the proposed approach

Rank	Team_Name	R-1	R-2	R-4	R-L	B-Pre	B-Rec	B-F1
1	Data Lovers	36.59	19.75	12.33	33.88	71.96	76.21	73.96
2	CSSG	34.21	17.13	10.20	3.12	74.10	73.43	73.71
3	Curious Coders	33.10	16.30	09.78	29.81	72.04	74.49	73.18
4	NIT_Patna	30.15	13.75	8.27	27.29	71.29	73.08	72.07

TABLE 5.8: Results on the testing dataset for Gujarati language using the proposed approach

Rank	Team_Name	R-1	R-2	R-4	R-L	B-Pre	B-Rec	B-F1
1	Data Lovers	27.92	14.96	9.42	26.69	75.06	73.01	73.98
2	Curious Coders	27.23	14.67	08.60	26.07	74.85	73.03	73.88
3	NIT_Patna	25.26	11.88	07.03	24.15	72.42	73.20	72.74
4	SynopSizers	21.09	08.35	04.37	19.58	75.78	68.44	71.86
5	Squad	18.10	08.11	03.47	17.48	69.29	73.01	71.05
6	SCaLAR	8.19	2.44	00.45	8.02	57.96	61.16	59.42
7	Trojan Horses	05.16	01.01	00.10	04.84	47.12	64.97	54.58

5.3.3 Conclusion

In this study, we applied TF-IDF and Singular Value Decomposition (SVD) techniques for extractive text summarization across various Indian languages. The

TABLE 5.9: Results on the testing dataset for Tamil language using the proposed approach

Rank	Team_Name	R-1	R-2	R-4	R-L	B-Pre	B-Rec	B-F1
1	Data Lovers	23.76	15.07	10.18	22.84	72.26	74.96	73.54
2	INITIATORS	2.18	13.36	09.05	20.91	73.01	72.92	72.90
3	Curious Coders	19.62	11.75	08.01	18.72	71.23	72.83	71.97
4	SynopSizers	15.47	08.77	05.61	14.68	66.06	72.92	69.25
5	NIT_Patna	13.92	07.50	04.87	13.34	68.67	70.51	69.48
6	Squad	01.21	00.07	00.01	01.20	61.92	57.47	59.51
7	SCaLAR	00.97	00.19	00.01	00.96	39.28	58.39	46.93

TABLE 5.10: Results on the testing dataset for Telugu language using the proposed approach

Rank	Team_Name	R-1	R-2	R-4	R-L	B-Pre	B-Rec	B-F1
1	INITIATORS	31.46	23.18	18.02	30.79	74.88	76.37	75.55
2	Data Lovers	30.22	21.49	16.06	29.63	75.44	75.27	75.32
3	Curious Coders	19.73	11.61	07.55	19.16	71.75	71.64	71.66
4	NIT_Patna	19.26	11.39	07.69	18.76	70.06	72.36	71.12
5	Squad	14.98	06.95	02.26	14.34	73.92	67.65	70.58

combined use of these methods provides valuable insights for generating higher-quality summaries by reducing redundancy and enhancing coherence. TF-IDF effectively identifies key terms based on their frequency and uniqueness within a document, while SVD captures latent semantic structures and relationships among words and sentences. When used together, TF-IDF highlights important content, and SVD reduces overlap by identifying semantically similar information, resulting in summaries that are both relevant and coherent.

Chapter 6

Abstractive Summarization of Indian English Using Transformer Architectures

The objectives of this chapter are following [1]:

- To introduce an efficient abstractive text summarization model using a sequence-to-sequence (Seq2Seq) architecture.
- To generate coherent and concise summaries that retain the source meaning from Indian English news articles in the ILSUM-2022 dataset.
- To evaluate the model performance using ROUGE metrics, aiming for improved ROUGE-1, ROUGE-2, ROUGE-3 and ROUGE-4 scores.

6.1 Introduction

The NLP research community has shown increasing interest in automatic text summarization for Indian languages. However, unlike widely spoken languages such as English, Chinese, French, and German-which benefit from large-scale, publicly available datasets-Indian languages lack such resources. Most existing

[1] The content of this chapter is based on [6]

datasets are either not publicly accessible or too limited in size to support effective research. To address this gap, The Forum for Information Retrieval Evaluation (FIRE) [138] organized the Indian Language Summarization (ILSUM) 2022 shared task, which provided datasets consisting of article-headline pairs sourced from leading newspapers across India. Each language dataset contains approximately 10,000 news articles. The objective of the task was to generate fixed-length summaries-either extractive or abstractivefor each article. In this study, we focus on all three languages offered in the ILSUM-2022 dataset: Hindi, English, and Gujarati, and details of these datasets are mentioned in Table 2.2 in chapter 2 [139]. To address this task, we developed deep learning-based encoder-decoder models for the Hindi, English and Gujarati datasets. Specifically, we implemented a sequence-to-sequence (Seq2Seq) architecture that employs a single-layer bidirectional long short-term memory (Bi-LSTM) network to encode the input text, and a single-layer unidirectional LSTM with global attention to decode and generate the summary. In this setup, the encoder captures the semantic representation of the input article as a fixed-length vector, which is then used by the decoder to generate a contextually relevant summary.

The rest of the paper is organized as follows: Section 6.2 describes the proposed framework for abstractive summarization. Section 6.3 outlines the experimental setup, results, and discussion. Finally, Section 6.4 provides the conclusion of the study.

6.2 Proposed Model

This section outlines the proposed methodology for abstractive summarization using a deep learning-based encoder-decoder framework. The encoder is built with a Bi-LSTM layer that captures contextual information and produces fixed-length feature representations, which are then passed to the attention mechanism and the decoder. The decoder leverages this information to extract the most relevant content, enabling the generation of coherent and informative summaries. The output from the decoder is further refined through a query vector and concatenation layers. Overall, the model is designed to produce multi-sentence abstractive summaries. The complete architecture is illustrated in Figure 6.1.

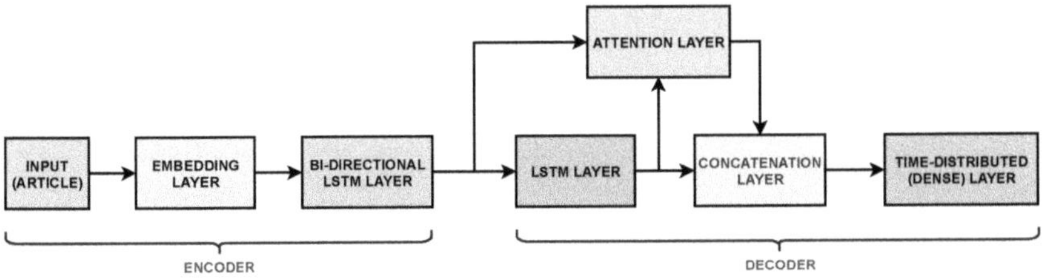

FIGURE 6.1: Proposed architecture diagram for the abstractive summarization.

6.2.1 Data Preprocessing

The data preprocessing phase consisted of two main steps, as illustrated in Figure 6.2. First, the entire text corpus was converted to lowercase to ensure uniformity. Next, unnecessary characters such as special symbols $\{@, \sim, ,,', \$\}$ were removed from the text using regular expression matching. These steps helped eliminate noise and resulted in a clean, standardized text corpus ready for further processing.

FIGURE 6.2: Different preprocessing steps.

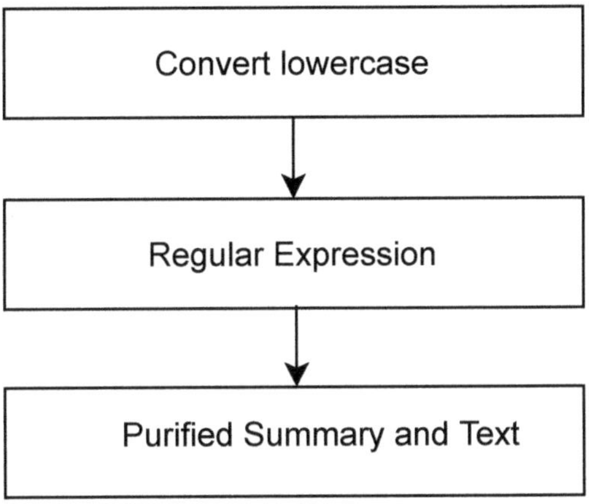

- **Convert lowercase**:- Converting words from uppercase to lowercase (e.g., "NLP" to "nlp") helps reduce redundancy in text representation. Although words like "Book" and "book" carry the same meaning, the vector space model treats them as separate tokens if their cases differ, leading to an unnecessarily larger feature space.

- **Regular Expression**:- Regular expressions, commonly referred to as RegEx, are sequences of characters used to identify, match, or replace specific patterns within text.

6.2.2 Word embedding

The significance of words in a text is influenced by both their frequency and semantic similarity. To enhance our model's performance, we experimented with various pre-trained word embedding models, including GloVe, ConceptNet Numberbatch, FastText, and Word2Vec . Among these, Word2Vec delivered the best results, and thus, we selected it for all subsequent tasks. In the article corpus, we observed that rare wordsdefined as those occurring exactly four timesaccounted for 1.88% of the total word frequency, and they made up 63.63% of the unique words. Based on this analysis, we removed all words with a frequency less than four from the article texts. Similarly, for the summary corpus, rare words with a frequency of six or fewer contributed to 8.26% of the total word coverage and comprised 77.37% of the vocabulary. Hence, we excluded words appearing fewer than six times in the summaries. These filtering steps were performed after initial text preprocessing. Removing such low-frequency words helps to reduce noise and ensures that the retained vocabulary is both meaningful and representative of the core content in the articles and summaries.

6.2.3 Encoder-Decoder

Recurrent Neural Networks (RNNs) have shown strong performance in sequence processing tasks, especially when handling input sequences of varying lengths [140]. Among RNN variants, Long Short-Term Memory (LSTM) networks often outperform standard or "vanilla" RNNs and are generally easier to train. Therefore, we employ an LSTM-based RNN as the encoder to generate a coarse representation of the input sequence [141]. LSTMs are well-suited for capturing dependencies across different time scales in a flexible and effective manner. These dependencies are modeled using the following set of equations. First, we recall the LSTM cell equations for a single direction. For time step t, input x_t previous hidden state $h_{t\text{-}1}$, and previous cell state $c_{t\text{-}1}$:

Gates and cell update:

$$\mathbf{i}_t = \sigma\left(\mathbf{W}_i \mathbf{x}_t + \mathbf{U}_i \mathbf{h}_{t-1} + \mathbf{b}_i\right) \tag{6.1}$$

$$\mathbf{f}_t = \sigma\left(\mathbf{W}_f \mathbf{x}_t + \mathbf{U}_f \mathbf{h}_{t-1} + \mathbf{b}_f\right) \tag{6.2}$$

$$\mathbf{o}_t = \sigma\left(\mathbf{W}_o \mathbf{x}_t + \mathbf{U}_o \mathbf{h}_{t-1} + \mathbf{b}_o\right) \tag{6.3}$$

$$\tilde{\mathbf{c}}_t = \tanh\left(\mathbf{W}_c \mathbf{x}_t + \mathbf{U}_c \mathbf{h}_{t-1} + \mathbf{b}_c\right) \tag{6.4}$$

$$\mathbf{c}_t = \mathbf{f}_t \odot \mathbf{c}_{t-1} + \mathbf{i}_t \odot \tilde{\mathbf{c}}_t \tag{6.5}$$

$$\mathbf{h}_t = \mathbf{o}_t \odot \tanh(\mathbf{c}_t) \tag{6.6}$$

Where,

- f_t denotes the forget gate
- i_t is the input gate
- o_t is the output gate
- c_t represents the cell state
- h_t is the hidden state
- $\sigma(\cdot)$ denotes the sigmoid function
- $\odot$ denotes element-wise multiplication

The matrices W_f, W_i, W_o, W_c and U_f, U_i, U_o, U_c are the learnable weight parameters of the network. Here, x_t refers to the input embedding vector at time step t, and h_t corresponds to the hidden state vector at the same time step.

The encoder is responsible for generating a fixed-length feature representation from the input sequence. To achieve this, a recurrent Bi-LSTM is employed, which captures contextual dependencies in both forward (left right) and backward (right left) directions, effectively modeling the full semantic relationships between words. The forward LSTM computes hidden state representations ($\overrightarrow{h_1}$, $\overrightarrow{h_2}$,... $\overrightarrow{h_j}$,... $\overrightarrow{h_m}$) at each word position sequentially in accordance with the current word embedding and the previous hidden state, given a sequence of the input word embeddings (i.e. $(x_1, x_2, x_j, ...x_m)$. For each word in reversed order, the backward LSTM generates hidden state representations ($\overleftarrow{h_1}$, $\overleftarrow{h_2}$,... $\overleftarrow{h_j}$,... $\overleftarrow{h_m}$) (i.e., from the last word to the first). The two different categories of hidden and cell states are

$$\overrightarrow{\mathbf{h}}_t = \mathrm{LSTM}_f\left(\mathbf{x}_t, \overrightarrow{\mathbf{h}}_{t-1}, \overrightarrow{\mathbf{c}}_{t-1}\right) \tag{6.7}$$

$$\overleftarrow{\mathbf{h}}_t = \mathrm{LSTM}_b\left(\mathbf{x}_t, \overleftarrow{\mathbf{h}}_{t+1}, \overleftarrow{\mathbf{c}}_{t+1}\right) \tag{6.8}$$

The final Bi-LSTM hidden representation at time step t is obtained by concatenating forward and backward states:

$$\mathbf{h}_t = \left[\overrightarrow{\mathbf{h}}_t ; \overleftarrow{\mathbf{h}}_t\right] \tag{6.9}$$

Next, we initialize the Bi-LSTM's states to zero vectors, with $\overrightarrow{h_1} = 0$ and $\overleftarrow{h_m} = 0$ as well as $\overrightarrow{c_1} = 0$ and $\overleftarrow{c_m} = 0$. Each word in the input sequence can be represented as a concatenated hidden state of a forward LSTM and a backward LSTM using the notation h_t=$[\overrightarrow{h_t}, \overleftarrow{h_t}]$. Similarly, indicate as c_t=$[\overrightarrow{c_t}, \overleftarrow{c_t}]$. We use LSTM as the decoder to generate the output summary. The encoder and decoder constitute a basic sequence-to-sequence model. Then, we connect the encoder to the decoder, by passing these states $[h_t, c_t]$.

We incorporate attention mechanism which takes the input from both encoder and decoder model as value and query respectively. In this regard, we give encoder output (h_t^e) and decoder output (h_t^d) to the attention layer.

$$\mathbf{at} = \mathrm{softmax}\left(\frac{\mathbf{h}_t^d \, \mathbf{h}_t^{e\top}}{\sqrt{d_{\mathbf{h}_t^e}}}\right) \tag{6.10}$$

where at is attention output.

The outputs from the attention and decoder layers are combined using a concatenation layer. This merged output is then fed into a TimeDistributed layer, which computes the probability distribution over the vocabulary for each word in the generated summary.

The probability of predicting the target word y_i at time step i, given the previous words y_1......, y_{i-1} and the input sequence x, is represented as:

$$P_v = P\left(y_i \mid y_1, y_2, \ldots, y_{i-1}, x\right) = \mathrm{softmax}\left(w_v \cdot px_i + b_v\right) \tag{6.11}$$

Here, px_i denotes the input from the previous layer at time step i, while w_v and b_v are the learnable weight and bias parameters. The softmax function is applied to compute the conditional probability distribution over the entire vocabulary.

6.2.4 Sequence to Sequence Model

Each sequence-to-sequence model comprises an encoder and a decoder, where the encoder is built using a Bi-LSTM and the decoder employs an LSTM architecture, as illustrated in Figure 6.3. The vocabulary is extended with special tokens such as PAD, EOS, and START. The PAD token is used to ensure that all sequences are padded to a uniform length. The EOS (End of Sequence) token indicates the termination of a sentence to the encoder, while the START token signals the decoder to initiate the decoding process.

In this context, the START and EOS tokens are selected from the dataset prior to training and are commonly used in sequence translation tasks. The encoder receives an input sequence denoted as x, and the decoder generates the corresponding output sequence denoted as y.

FIGURE 6.3: End-to-end sequence to sequence model

6.3 Experiment setup, Results and Discussion

This section presents the experimental setup used in our study, followed by a detailed of results obtained. We also interpreted and explained the meaning of the results in discussion section.

6.3.1 Experimental setting

We implemented the proposed sequence-to-sequence model using TensorFlow [142], version 2.9.1. This model consisted of two parts: (1) encoder, (2) decoder. The encoder is a Bi-LSTM with a hidden state dimension of 128, while the decoder is an LSTM with a hidden dimension of 256. A word embedding size of 300 was used to represent the input tokens. Once the training phase is complete, the model is capable of generating summaries autonomously. The output summary length is fixed at 75 tokens. Following extensive evaluation and hyperparameter tuning, the final model was trained using the RMSprop optimizer [143] and the sparse categorical crossentropy loss function, which provided faster and more stable convergence. The training was performed over 50 epochs with a batch size of 32 and a learning rate of 0.001. The regularization techniques employed to prevent overfitting (such as dropout and early stopping) have now been clearly specified. This model was evaluated using the ILSUM-2022 dataset. As described in Table 2.2, the dataset was split in an 80:20 ratio, with 80% of the samples used for training the model and the remaining 20% used for testing its performance.

6.3.2 Results

This section presents the results obtained on the validation and test datasets provided by ILSUM-2022 [139], as outlined in Table 2.2 in Chapter 2. The performance of the proposed model on the validation datasets for Hindi, English, and Gujarati using the ROUGE-1 metric is shown in Table 6.1. At this stage, the model utilized embeddings from a pre-trained language model without updating the embedding weights during training (i.e., trainable=False). As a result, the overall number of trainable parameters in the end-to-end network was reduced, as illustrated in Figure 6.1.

The results obtained on the English test dataset are presented in Table 6.2. These results were generated after enabling embedding fine-tuning during backpropagation (trainable=True). Evaluation metrics including precision, recall, and F1-score were computed for ROUGE-1 through ROUGE-4. ROUGE-1 evaluates unigram (1-gram) overlap, whereas ROUGE-4 considers 4-gram overlap. As expected, the ROUGE scores tend to decrease with increasing n-gram size due to the increased difficulty in matching longer sequences. Among these, our proposed model performs best on the ROUGE-1 metric, indicating strong performance in capturing key individual words from the reference summaries.

6.3.3 Discussion

In this section, we now included a dedicated discussion on factual consistency in the abstractive model, where we analyze common error patterns such as hallucination, content omission, and incorrect entity references. To evaluate factual reliability, we complemented automatic evaluation metrics (e.g., ROUGE) with a qualitative human judgment analysis on a representative subset of generated summaries. Human evaluators assessed the summaries with respect to factual correctness, faithfulness to the source text, and semantic consistency. Additionally, we used of attention mechanisms within the Seq2Seq framework helps mitigate factual errors by encouraging better alignment between source content and generated summaries.

Indian English differs from standard varieties (e.g., American or British English) in multiple linguistic aspects: Vocabulary and Lexical Choices, Syntax and Grammar Variations, Spelling and Orthography, Pragmatics and Politeness Markers, Code-Mixing. Pre-trained language models like BERT, GPT, or RoBERTa are typically trained on standard English corpora, such as Wikipedia, news articles, or Common Crawl data. Specifically, our focus was on evaluating lightweight and computationally efficient approaches suitable for resource-constrained environments, where transformer-based models may be impractical due to their high computational and memory requirements.

TABLE 6.1: Results on Hindi, English, and Gujarati Validation Dataset for ROUGE-1 metric

Validation Datasets	Precision	Recall	F1-score
Hindi	0.294781	0.215508	0.238898
Gujarati	0.000111	0.000281	.000158
English	0.000616	0.000465	0.000961

TABLE 6.2: Results on English Dataset for ROUGE-1, ROUGE-2, ROUGE-3 and ROUGE-4

English TestData	Precision	Recall	F1-score
ROUGE-1	0.356147961	0.326064401	0.328213556
ROUGE-2	0.176917204	0.166501352	0.165805031
ROUGE-3	0.129456619	0.123251567	0.122045746
ROUGE-4	0.103489988	0.099644622	0.09809286

6.4 Conclusion

We enhance the traditional sequence-to-sequence (Seq2Seq) framework for abstractive text summarization by introducing an effective English-to-English summarization approach that employs a Bi-LSTM encoder and an LSTM decoder with word2vec text reprsentation technique. Our model builds upon a standard encoder-decoder architecture, augmented with an attention mechanism to improve performance. Comprehensive experiments on the ILSUM-2022 English dataset show that the proposed model achieves competitive, state-of-the-art results in generating high-quality summaries.

Chapter 7

Conclusion and Future Research Directions

The objectives of the chapter are:

1. To summarize the research findings and contributions.
2. To discuss how these contributions address the research gaps.
3. To present a detailed discussion of the research gap in Chapter 1.
4. To discuss limitations of the thesis and future directions of current research.

7.1 Introduction

This chapter concludes the thesis by summarizing the major findings and contributions made through the study. It also outlines future research directions, demonstrating how the proposed work can advance the field of text summarization. The aim of this research was to design an automatic summarization for multiple low resource and code-mixing languages.

To achieve this, the study was guided by four research gap formulated in Chapter 1, which were derived from in Chapter 2.

1 To design a system for generating error free, and more coherent extractive summary using a supervised PSO and dynamic PSO framework

by introducing an Incorrect word and Fluency Score for enhanced accuracy, as motivated by RG 3

2 To design a system for generating the extractive summary using machine learning (ML) regression models with Node2Vec feature, as motivated by RG 1.

3 To design a system for generating extractive summary using statistical, and linguistic features for low resource Indian languages, as motivated by RG 2.

4 To develop an encoder-decoder-based system for generating abstractive summaries specifically tailored to the Indian English language, as motivated by RG 4.

7.2 Thesis contribution

This thesis introduces a range of statistical, optimization, machine learning and deep learning approaches for comprehensive text summarization analysis in four dimensions : generating error-free and more meaning full summaries in standard English, addressing challenges like morophology, polysemy in low-resource and code-mixed languages such as Hindi and Gujarati for, Also extracting statistical and linguistic features for Indian English and Hindi and other seven low resource languages. This thesis also developed abstractive summarization framework for Indian English.

In next, we dicussed how each of the above mentioned objectives has been successfully achieved through the proposed models in the following subdivisions.

7.2.1 To design a system for generating error free extractive summary using a supervised PSO and dynamic PSO framework by introducing an Incorrect word" and Fluency Score for enhanced accuracy.

In Chapter 3, we developed two extractive summarization models for the English language. In the first approach, we proposed a novel method, XSumm-PSO, where each sentence is represented using ten features. Sentence scores are computed based on these features with appropriate weights that indicate the relative importance of each feature and guide the summary generation process. The summaries produced by this method captured a substantial portion of the relevant content while avoiding the inclusion of "Incorrect word," as compared to human-authored summaries. In this approach, 30% of the sentences were extracted from the original document to form the final summary. The comparative results of the proposed XSumm-PSO model against the baseline models (as discussed in Section 3.2.2) are presented in Tables 3.8, and 3.9, corresponding to DUC-2002, and CNN/DailyMail datasets, respectively.

In the second approach, we introduced XSumm-DPSO, an enhanced method where each sentence is represented using nineteen distinct features. Sentence importance is assessed through weighted evaluation, with the weights reflecting the significance of each feature. These weights play a critical role in producing more grammatically sound summaries using "Fluency Score" . As with the previous method, the top 30% of sentences were selected to construct the summaries. When benchmarked against several state-of-the-art techniques, the proposed XSumm-DPSO approach demonstrated superior performance. Moreover, the summaries generated were found to be both coherent and easily comprehensible by readers. The comparative results of the proposed XSumm-DPSO model against the baseline models are presented in Tables 3.14 and 3.13, corresponding to DUC-2002 and CNN/DailyMail datasets, respectively. To ensure the robustness of the results, statistical tests were also conducted, confirming the consistency of the outcomes across multiple iterations.

7.2.2 To design a system for generating the extractive summary using ML regression models with node2vec feature

In Chapter 4, we introduced and implemented a multilingual extractive text summarization framework named XSumm-ML_RFR . This approach leverages Node2Vec embeddings as the core feature representation to capture rich semantic and structural properties of the input text. The Node2Vec algorithm, inspired by a combination of random walks and the Word2Vec model, effectively learns continuous feature representations for nodes (i.e., sentences or tokens) in a text graph.

These representations are particularly beneficial for modeling contextual dependencies and semantic similarities, which are essential for generating high-quality summaries.

To assess the effectiveness of Node2Vec-based features for extractive summarization, we experimented with several machine learning regression models to assign importance scores to individual sentences. Among them, the Random Forest Regressor (RFR) consistently delivered superior performance in terms of ROUGE-1, ROUGE-2, and ROUGE-L scores across multiple language datasets. The evaluation results on the DUC 2002 dataset are detailed in Table 4.11 at a 40% compression rate. The proposed XSumm_ML-RFR-Node2Vec model outperformed several state-of-the-art (SOTA) methods, with comparative results for Hindi and Gujarati languages presented in Table 4.10 at same compression rate.

The XSumm-ML_RFR model was rigorously tested on multilingual datasets covering three Indian languages, and summaries were generated at four different compression rates: 40%, 30%, 20%, and 10%. The detailed results, illustrating the models effectiveness in preserving informativeness and reducing redundancy, are comprehensively presented in Tables 4.6, 4.7, 4.8, and 4.9. This approach demonstrates the viability of combining graph-based embeddings with machine learning regression techniques for extractive summarization in a multilingual context.

7.2.3 To design a system for generating extractive summary using statistical, and linguistic features for low resource Indian languages

In Chapter 5, two approaches are presented. In the first approach, we developed effective XSumm-TenAF framework to create extractive text summarizers, achieving success in both Hindi and English summarization tasks. The framework is built on ten handcrafted features named: Sentence Position , Sentence Length , sentence numeric , Sentence Thematic , Sentence Entropy , PosTag (noun and verb), TF-ISF , Sentenc Aggregation , Busy Path , and Title Match . The evaluation of proposed model is conducted on the ILSUM-2022 datasets (comprising both English and Hindi data). It shows that the XSumm-TenAF produce noteworthy results in Tables 5.1 and 5.2 at 10%, 15% and 20% compression rates.

In the second approach, we combined TF-IDF and SVD for extractive summarization across Indian languages. TF-IDF helped identify key terms based on their importance, while SVD captured underlying semantic relationships. Together, these techniques reduced redundancy and improved the coherence of the summaries, leading to more relevant and informative outputs. The performance of the proposed model on the training dataset across seven languages -Telugu, Tamil, Kannada, Hindi, English, Gujarati, and Bengali-is presented in Table 5.4. Additionally, the models performance on the validation dataset for five languages -Telugu, Tamil, Kannada, Hindi, and Englishis shown in Table 5.5. The performance of proposed model on the test datasets for Bengali, Hindi, Gujarati, Tamil, and Telugu are presented in Tables 5.6, 5.7, 5.8, 5.9, and 5.10, respectively. We achieved the 3rd position in the Bengali and Gujarati language categories on the test datasets for Task 1, under the team name Sangita_NIT_Patna (NIT_Patna).

7.2.4 To develop an encoder-decoder-based system for generating abstractive summaries specifically tailored to the Indian English language

In Chapter 6, we present the development of an encoder-decoder-based deep learning model specifically tailored for generating abstractive summaries in the Indian English language domain. The architecture of the proposed model is grounded in the classical sequence-to-sequence (Seq2Seq) framework, consisting of an encoder and a decoder, and further enhanced with an attention mechanism to dynamically focus on the most relevant parts of the input during decoding.

To capture the semantic and syntactic features of the input text effectively, we utilize Word2Vec embeddings as the input representations. These pretrained embeddings enable the model to understand word-level relationships and contextual similarities, which are essential for generating coherent and contextually appropriate summaries. The model was trained and evaluated on a curated dataset of Indian English texts. Its performance was assessed using standard evaluation metrics from the ROUGE family. The proposed model attained F_1-scores of 0.32, 0.16, 0.12, and 0.09 for ROUGE-1, ROUGE-2, ROUGE-3, and ROUGE-4, respectively. These scores reflect the models ability to capture not only individual keywords but also bi-grams, tri-grams, and higher-order n-gram structures that are critical for evaluating abstractive summaries. The results demonstrate that the model, despite its simplicity, is capable of generating meaningful summaries for Indian English content.

7.3 Limitations

While the research presented in this thesis contributes meaningfully to the field of text summarization. It also demonstrate promising results, several limitations remains that may affect the generalizability and scope of for further exploration:

- **Language and Dataset Constraints:** Although the models have been evaluated on multiple Indian languages and benchmark datasets, the performance may not fully generalize to low-resource or underrepresented dialects due to limited annotated data and linguistic variation.
- **Focus on Single-Document Summarization:** This work primarily addresses single-document summarization, and does not extend to multi-document summarization, which is more complex and relevant for news aggregation, legal summaries, or scientific reviews.
- **Evaluation Metrics Bias:** The reliance on traditional metrics ROUGE such as ROUGE-1, ROUGE-2, and ROUGE-L presents a limitation. These metrics emphasize n-gram overlap and often fail to capture semantic meaning, grammatical fluency, and factual consistency.
- **Abstractive Model Limitations:** Transformer-based abstractive summarizers, although powerful, are prone to generating hallucinated content-i.e., information that is fluent but not grounded in the source text. This affects the factual reliability of summaries.
- **Computational Cost and Resource Requirements:** Advanced summarization models, particularly transformer-based architectures like LongT5, are computationally expensive and require significant training time and hardware resources, limiting accessibility and real-world deployment in low-resource settings. In the extractive approaches (e.g., XSumm-PSO , XSumm-DPSO , ML models), summary quality is influenced by manually selected features. This may limit scalability and adaptability across different domains without further tuning.

- **Absence of Robustness and Bias Testing:** The summarization models have not been rigorously tested against adversarial inputs, nor has the thesis addressed potential biases in training data or outputs, which are critical concerns in real-world applications.

7.4 Future Directions

Building upon the current work and addressing the limitations highlighted, several promising directions emerge for future research in the domain of text summarization. we have reorganized the future directions into two subsections:

- The immediate next steps involve extensions that build directly upon the current thesis framework and can be pursued in the short term. One important direction is the expansion of the proposed summarization approach to low-resource Indian languages and code-mixed text, which are common in real-world multilingual settings.

  To address the limitations of ROUGE-based evaluation metrics, future work should adopt more comprehensive evaluation protocols. This includes incorporating semantic similarity measures such as BERTScore and QuestEval, along with structured human evaluation frameworks that assess fluency, informativeness, and factual correctness. Such evaluations would provide a more reliable assessment of summary quality beyond surface-level n-gram overlap.

  Enhancing model fairness, robustness, and safety also constitutes a critical future direction. This involves evaluating summarization models under adversarial inputs and systematically auditing them for potential demographic, linguistic, or topical biases. Additionally, initial efforts toward hallucination mitigation in abstractive summarization should be expanded. Future research can focus on integrating factual consistency modules, such as verification networks, grounding mechanisms, or external knowledge sources, to reduce hallucinated content in transformer-based abstractive models.

  Finally, the integration of deep semantic representations presents a valuable opportunity for further improvement. While handcrafted features offer interpretability, combining them with contextual embeddings from pretrained multilingual models such as mBERT, IndicBERT, and XLM-R can significantly enrich sentence representations. This hybrid feature space has the potential to improve both extractive and abstractive summarization performance, particularly in multilingual and low-resource scenarios.

- The long-term research agenda envisions broader and more ambitious extensions of the proposed work to address emerging challenges and real-world requirements in automatic summarization. One key direction is the development of cross-lingual and multilingual summarization systems that can effectively operate across multiple languages, enabling knowledge transfer from high-resource languages to low-resource ones. Closely related to this is the exploration of domain adaptation techniques, allowing models trained on high-resource domains such as news to be efficiently adapted to low-resource and specialized domains, including medical, legal, and scientific texts, with minimal re-training.

  Another significant avenue is multi-document summarization, which is essential for applications such as news aggregation, legal case analysis, and systematic literature reviews. Future models should be capable of summarizing information from multiple documents by capturing diverse perspectives, reducing redundancy, and maintaining coherence and factual consistency across sources. Extending beyond single-modality text summarization, future research can also focus on multimodal summarization, where information from text, images, audio, and video is jointly processed to generate richer and more informative summaries that better reflect real-world content.

  To ensure practical applicability, research should also emphasize resource-efficient summarization models. Developing lightweight, compressed, or distilled models can significantly reduce computational and memory requirements, making summarization systems deployable in low-resource environments such as mobile devices, edge computing platforms, and rural digital centers.

  Finally, interactive and user-centered summarization represents a promising long-term goal. Future systems could incorporate user intent modeling and interactive feedback mechanisms to generate personalized summaries tailored to individual user needs. Such systems would allow users to dynamically control summary length, style, level of detail, or focus areas, thereby enhancing usability, transparency, and user satisfaction. Collectively, these directions aim to advance summarization systems toward being more adaptable, efficient, fair, and aligned with real-world user expectations.

www.ingramcontent.com/pod-product-compliance
Lightning Source LLC
LaVergne TN
LVHW051922051126
851857LV00021B/2104